It's So Easy...

Kitchen Memories
Cookbook

All your children shall be taught by the Lord,
And great shall be the peace of your children.
Isaiah 54:13 (NKJV)

It's So Easy...

Kitchen Memories Cookbook

Your Recipe for Family Fun
in the Kitchen

by Sheila Simmons

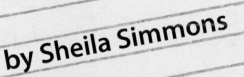

Great American Publishers

www.GreatAmericanPublishers.com

TOLL-FREE 1-888-854-5954

To my boys of yesterday and tomorrow—
Ryan, Nic, and Trace, and the love of my life who gets
all the credit for this book, Roger.

Great American Publishers

171 Lone Pine Church Road • Lena, MS 39094

toll-free 1-888-854-5954 • www.GreatAmericanPublishers.com

ISBN 978-1-934817-26-1

10 9 8 7 6 5 4 3 2

by Sheila Simmons

Front Cover: Images ©James Stefuik: Frog Cupcakes, p181; Finger Paint, p198
Images © istock.com by the creator noted: laminate countertop, Roel Smart; girl chef, Dejan Ristovski;
rabbit cooking pancake, Alexeyzet; asparagus crown, valbar

Back Cover: Images ©James Stefuik: Monster Mouths, p121; Happy Ice Cream Mice, p233; Popcorn Cake, p158; Hand Print, p142
Images © istock.com by the creator noted: popcorn scatter, tanjichica7; crayons, empire331

All other image credits listed on page 254.

To purchase books in quantity for corporate use, incentives, or fundraising,
please call Great American Publishers at 1-888-854-5954.

Contents

Introduction

My children are grown now. Ryan is married; he and his wife Shelbie are expecting their first child. Nicholas will soon be graduating high school and moving on to the next phase of his life.

Yet, it seems like yesterday my house was full of young and always boisterous boys. I have two sons by birth, but my house has always been full of myriad boys—hanging out, always grabbing a bite to eat, and always bringing life and joy to the house.

I so miss those days that I encourage everyone, while your children are young, to cherish the busy and often loud times for they are fleeting. And this is what makes *Kitchen Memories Cookbook* so special. Like children in the house, this book is fun and lively and a little loud.

Kitchen Memories Cookbook is not your average memory book. I call it "free-style" because the memories are not in chronological order. Actually, they are not in any order at all. Instead, this book is a chaotic, fun collection of memories all jumbled up with recipes for dishes your family will love and arts and craft ideas your family will enjoy.

We've included a space to record the name and date for each memory so you can use this book with your whole family, each of your children individually, your grandchildren (as I will be doing soon) or even your nieces and nephews… any child you love. It's the perfect way to entertain the kids while making a lifetime of memories for both of you. And when those days are done, you will have a cherished family keepsake to keep forever and hand down through generations.

However you decide to use the book, there is just one requirement… HAVE FUN!

Happy Memories to you and yours,

Sheila Simmons

I ❤ CIDER!

Red Hot Cider

½ gallon apple cider
½ cup red hot cinnamon candies

Pour apple cider into a large pot or teapot, add red hots. Heat and stir until candy has melted and cider has turned red. Pour into 8 mugs and serve hot. Makes 8 servings.

Ocean in a Bottle

Large clear plastic soda bottle
Water
Vegetable Oil
Blue or green food coloring

Rinse bottle, and remove all labels. Fill half full of water and then a quarter full of oil. Add a few drops of food coloring. Tightly replace top. Rock, roll, and make waves!

Summer Punch

1 (32-ounce) bottle cranberry juice
1 (32-ounce) bottle apple juice
½ cup lemon juice
1 quart ginger ale
Ice

Mix all ingredients in punch bowl. Serve on a hot summer day for a cool treat.

LEMONADE
10¢

Have you ever had a lemonade stand?

Draw a picture of your stand or what your stand would look like . . .

Name_____ Age_____

Homemade Lemonade

1 lemon
1 cup cold water
2 teaspoons sugar or to taste
Ice cubes

Juice lemon by squeezing by hand or using a juicer. Strain to remove seeds and pulp. Add water and sugar; mix. Pour into 2 glasses; add ice cubes.

Orange you thirsty?

Cut or bite the end off a soft peppermint stick. Make a small slit in an orange, insert the peppermint stick, then sip the juice through your sweet straw.

Lemon-Orange Frosty

1 (8-ounce) carton lowfat lemon yogurt
½ cup orange juice
4 ice cubes

Combine yogurt and orange juice in a blender. Process 30 seconds. Drop ice cubes in one at a time, processing 30 seconds after each. With last ice cube, process until smooth. Makes 2 cups.

Apple Banana Frosty

1 Golden Delicious apple, diced
1 banana, peeled and sliced
¼ cup milk
3 ice cubes

Blend all ingredients in blender until smooth; serve immediately. Makes 1 serving.

Purple Cow Shakes

1 (6-ounce) can frozen grape juice
   concentrate
1 cup milk
2 cups vanilla ice cream

Pour juice concentrate and milk into blender. Add ice cream. Cover and blend on high speed for 30 seconds. Serve right away. Makes 3 to 4 shakes.

Maple Milk Shake

1 pint chocolate ice cream, softened
1 quart cold milk
½ cup maple syrup

Place ice cream, milk and syrup in mixer bowl. Beat with electric mixer. Pour into glasses. Serve cold.

What is your best Christmas memory?

Peppermint Float

2 tablespoons finely crushed peppermint candy
1 quart peppermint ice cream
4 cups milk

Combine candy, milk and ½ of ice cream in large mixer bowl. Beat on low speed until slushy. Pour into chilled glasses. Top each with a scoop of remaining ice cream. Makes 6 servings.

Name _____

Age _____

PRINCIPAL

Have you ever been to the principal's office?

☐ **Yes** ☐ **No**

Name_____

Grade_____

Banana Cheesecake Dip

½ cup sour cream
2 ounces cream cheese
2 tablespoons plus 1 teaspoon milk
2 tablespoons sugar
½ teaspoon vanilla
Nutmeg (optional)
6 medium bananas, unpeeled and cut crosswise into halves

Blend all ingredients, except nutmeg and bananas, until smooth. Refrigerate until ready to serve. Before serving, sprinkle top with nutmeg, if desired. Partially peel bananas and dip directly into Cheesecake Dip. Makes 6 servings.

Tropical Coconut Cream Dipping Sauce: Substitute coconut extract for vanilla.

Write about your trip to the principal's office . . .

Can you name all the states?

Which is your favorite state to visit?

_____

Name_____ Age_____

Which states have you visited?

Color in each state as you go!

☐ **Yes** ☐ **No**

Texas Trash Warm Bean Dip

1 (8-ounce) package cream cheese, softened
1 cup sour cream
2 (16-ounce) cans refried beans
1 packet taco seasoning
2 cups shredded Cheddar cheese
2 cups shredded Monterey Jack cheese

Preheat oven to 350°. Mix cream cheese and sour cream in a large bowl. Add refried beans and taco seasoning; mix until well combined. Spread mixture in greased 9x13-inch baking pan. Sprinkle with both cheeses. Bake 25 to 30 minutes, or until cheese is melted and slightly browned. Serve with tortilla chips.

Chili Billies

40 tortilla or corn chips
½ cup shredded cheese
½ can chili

Place chips on a large microwave-safe plate, then sprinkle cheese on top. Add chili, and microwave 1 minutes. May layer or make several small plates.

Broccoli Cheese Quesadillas

1 cup shredded Cheddar cheese
½ cup finely chopped fresh broccoli
2 tablespoons picante sauce or salsa
4 (6- to 7-inch) corn or flour tortillas
2 teaspoons butter or margarine, divided

Combine cheese, broccoli and picante sauce in small bowl; mix well. Spoon ¼ of mixture onto each tortilla; fold tortilla over filling. Melt 1 teaspoon butter in large nonstick skillet over medium heat. Add 2 quesadillas; cook about 2 minutes on each side or until tortillas are golden brown and cheese is melted. Repeat with remaining butter and quesadillas. Cool completely. Makes 4 servings.

Jalapeño Popper Dip

Everyone will ask for your recipe!

6 to 8 slices bacon, diced and cooked crispy

2 (8-ounces) packages of cream cheese, softened

1 cup mayonnaise

4 to 6 jalapeños, deseeded and chopped (The seeds will make it fiery hot. Be careful not to touch seeds or jalapeños with your bare hands.)

1 cup shredded Cheddar cheese

½ cup shredded mozzarella cheese

¼ cup diced green onion

Preheat oven to 350°. Combine ingredients in a medium bowl. Stir well. Transfer to a 1-quart baking dish.

TOPPING:

1 cup crushed Ritz crackers

½ cup grated Parmesan cheese

½ stick butter, melted

Combine Topping ingredients and sprinkle on top of dip. Bake 20 to 30 minutes or until bubbly. Serve with tortilla chips or corn chips.

What is your pet's name?

Name _____

Age _____

Corn Dog Twists

1 (11-ounce) can breadsticks (the twist and bake dough)

8 hot dogs

⅛ cup Parmesan cheese

⅛ cup cornmeal

½ stick margarine, melted

Unroll dough and separate breadsticks. Cut half of the breadsticks in half. Wrap each hot dog with 1½ strips. Combine Parmesan cheese and cornmeal. Brush butter over each wrapped dog and cover with a very light coating of Parmesan cheese or cornmeal. Makes 8 servings.

Dogs in a Blanket

10 wieners
Cheese
1 (10-count) can biscuits

Preheat oven to 375°. Split each wiener lengthwise, but not completely through. Slice cheese to fit into slit of wiener. Flatten each biscuit; place 1 wiener on each flattened biscuit. Roll biscuit around wiener; secure with toothpick. Place on cookie sheet. Bake 10 minutes or until biscuits are browned. Makes 10 servings.

Make Your Own Pizza Shapes

1 (13.8-ounce) package refrigerated pizza dough
¼ to ½ cup prepared pizza sauce
1 cup shredded mozzarella cheese
1 cup French's French Fried Onions

Preheat oven to 425°. Unroll dough onto a cutting board. Press or roll dough into 12x8-inch rectangle. With sharp knife or pizza cutter, cut dough into large shape of your choice (butterfly, heart, star). Reroll any scraps and cut into mini shapes. Place dough on greased baking sheet. Pre-bake 7 minutes or until crust just begins to brown. Spread with sauce and top with cheese. Bake 6 minutes or until crust is deep golden brown. Sprinkle with French Fried Onions. Bake 2 minutes longer or until golden. Makes 4 to 6 servings

Pizza Snacks

6 English muffins
1 (14-ounce) jar pizza sauce
1 (8-ounce) package sliced pepperoni
1 (8-ounce) package shredded mozzarella cheese

Halve muffins lengthwise; spread each half with pizza sauce; top with pepperoni and cheese. Bake at 350° until cheese melts.

Variation: Use olives and cut-up veggies to decorate with faces or other designs.

What do you want to be when you grow up?

_____

Name_____ Age_____

Draw something you would use in your job.

Cheese Pops

1 (8-ounce) package cream cheese, softened
½ cup raisins
1 cup wheat germ
Pretzel sticks

Beat cream cheese with a spoon or mixer; add raisins and mix well. Roll into small balls (the size of a large grape) and roll in wheat germ. Insert a pretzel stick in to each pop for a "handle." Store in refrigerator. Makes about 20.

Egg Sailboats

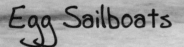

12 hard-cooked eggs
½ cup mayonnaise
1 teaspoon mustard
2 dozen flat toothpicks
2 dozen triangle shaped pieces of sliced cheese

Shell eggs, slice in halves, and remove yolks. Combine yolks with mayonnaise and mustard and return a spoonful of mixture to the hollow of each egg white. Make a sail for each boat (egg half) by stringing a slice of cheese onto a toothpick to make a sail on a mast. Poke each into an egg half. This snack will sail into the mouths of your hungry snackers. Be sure they remove the masts (toothpicks) before eating.

Ants on a Log

This fun snack will have you welcoming ants into your kitchen.

½ cup creamy peanut butter
1 (5-ounce) jar process cheese spread
3 stalks celery, cut into 2 inch pieces
Raisins

Combine peanut butter and cheese spread, blending thoroughly. Fill each celery piece with a heaping spoonful of mixture. Arrange raisin "ants" on each "log." Refrigerate, storing in plastic container.

Variation: Spread plain cream cheese or peanut butter onto celery.

Draw a garden!

Name_____ Age_____

Make a Crystal Garden

4 tablespoons non-iodized salt
4 tablespoons distilled water
1 tablespoon ammonia

Charcoal
Colored inks (optional)

Mix salt, water and ammonia; pour over several pieces of charcoal in a plastic bowl or container. Put several drops of ink on the charcoal pieces. Leave the bowl in a place where it will be undisturbed and over several days, crystals will begin to form. To keep your garden growing, every few days add another mixture of the first three ingredients directly into the bottom of the container (don't pour directly onto crystal garden).

Favorite thing to do inside.

Name _____

Age _____

Cheesy-O's

⅓ cup butter or margarine
⅓ cup grated Parmesan
    cheese
5 cups Cheerios

Heat oven to 300°. Melt butter in a 9x13-inch baking pan. Stir in Parmesan cheese. Add Cheerios and mix well. Bake, uncovered, 10 minutes. Makes 5 cups. Spice these up by adding paprika or seasoned salt to taste.

Bugs in a Boat

1 (5-ounce) jar pineapple cheese spread, softened
3 apples, cored and cut into 6 wedges each
Golden raisins

Top each apple wedge with a heaping teaspoon pineapple cheese spread. Arrange golden raisin "bugs" on top. Serves 9.

Nuts and Bolts

A zesty snack for your hard working kid.

1½ cups Kix cereal
1 cup Cheerios cereal
2 cups cheese crackers
2 cups pretzels
½ pound mixed nuts
¼ cup melted margarine
½ teaspoon Worcestershire sauce
¼ teaspoon garlic salt
¼ teaspoon celery salt

Mix cereals, crackers, pretzels, and nuts in shallow baking pan. Combine melted margarine, Worcestershire and salts. Pour over cereal mixture and gently stir. Bake at 250° for 30 minutes, stirring after 15 minutes. Makes 6 cups.

Where was your first vacation?

_____

Name_____

Age _____

What was your favorite part?

_____

Traveling Tidbits

A tasty and easy-to-eat snack perfect for a day hike or long car trips.

2 cups roasted, unsalted peanuts
¾ cup raisins
½ cup dried apples, chopped
½ cup dried apricots, chopped
1 cup chipped coconut
½ cup sunflower seeds
½ cup walnuts

Mix everything together in a big bowl. Store covered in a cool place until you're ready to travel.

Bear Bite Snack Mix

2 teaspoons sugar
¾ teaspoon ground cinnamon
¼ teaspoon ground nutmeg
1½ cups sweetened corn or oat cereal squares
1 cup teddy bear-shaped graham crackers
1 cup raisins
½ cup dried fruit bits or chopped mixed dried fruit

Preheat oven to 350°. Combine sugar, cinnamon and nutmeg in small bowl; mix well. Combine cereal, graham crackers, raisins and dried fruit bits on jellyroll pan. Generously spray with cooking spray. Sprinkle with half of sugar mixture; mix well. Spray again with cooking spray; sprinkle with remaining sugar mixture. Bake 5 minutes; stir. Bake 5 minutes more; stir. Cool completely in pan on wire rack. Store in airtight container. Makes 4 cups.

Tell me about your favorite toy.

_____

_____

Name _____

Age _____

Muddy Buddies

9 cups Chex cereal (Corn, Rice, Wheat, Double, or Multi-Bran)
1 cup chocolate chips
½ cup peanut butter
¼ cup (½ stick) margarine, softened
¼ teaspoon vanilla
1½ cups powdered sugar

Place cereal in large bowl and set aside. Melt chocolate chips, peanut butter and margarine over medium heat, stirring until well combined. Add vanilla. Pour over cereal, stirring until evenly coated, then pour cereal mixture into a large bag with powdered sugar. Shake until all pieces are well coated. Spread on waxed paper to cool. Store in airtight container.

Brontosaurus Bites

4 cups popped popcorn
2 cups mini-dinosaur grahams
2 cups Corn Chex cereal
1½ cups dried pineapple wedges
1 (6-ounce) package dried fruit bits
1 tablespoon plus 1½ teaspoons sugar
1½ teaspoons ground cinnamon
½ teaspoon ground nutmeg
1 cup yogurt-covered raisins

Preheat oven to 350°. Combine popcorn, grahams, cereal, pineapple and fruit bits in large bowl. Transfer to 10x15-inch jellyroll pan. Spray mixture generously with cooking spray. Combine sugar, cinnamon and nutmeg in small bowl. Sprinkle half of sugar mixture over popcorn mixture; toss lightly to coat. Spray mixture again with cooking spray. Sprinkle with remaining sugar mixture; mix lightly. Bake 10 minutes, stirring after 5 minutes. Cool completely in pan on wire rack. Add raisins; mix lightly. Makes 12 (¾ cup) servings.

What is your favorite movie? Why?

Nutty Popcorn

A delicious handheld treat perfect for your child's lunch box.

1½ quarts unsalted popcorn
1 cup salted peanuts
½ cup seedless raisins
½ cup sugar

½ cup light corn syrup
½ cup creamy peanut butter
½ teaspoon vanilla extract

In large mixing bowl, combine popcorn, peanuts and raisins. In heavy medium saucepan, combine sugar and corn syrup; bring to a rolling boil, stirring constantly. Remove from heat and stir in peanut butter and vanilla. Pour syrup over popcorn mixture and toss lightly to coat evenly. Press into well-buttered muffin pan cups. Let stand until firm; remove and serve in paper cupcake liners.

Homemade Microwave Popcorn

⅓ cup popcorn kernels
2 to 3 tablespoons melted butter

Salt

Pour kernels into standard lunch size paper bag and fold top of bag over twice to close (each fold should be ½ inch deep; remember the kernels need room to pop). Seal bag with 2 pieces of tape placed 2 to 3 inches apart. Place bag in microwave on carousel. Cook on high 2 to 3 minutes, or until the pops are 5 seconds apart.

Name _____

Age _____

Where do you prefer to watch movies?

☐ at the theater
☐ at home
☐ in the car

Granny Goose Popcorn

1 cup sugar
3 tablespoons water
¼ cup butter
1 tablespoon vanilla
Food coloring

Boil all ingredients 2 to 3 minutes. Pour over popped corn.

If I had a pet monkey:

_____

_____

Name_____ Age_____

4-Ingredient Banana Bread

1 box yellow cake mix
2 eggs
4 or 5 overripe bananas
1¾ cups chocolate chips

Add all ingredients to a large bowl or stand mixer and mix well. Fill 2 medium, greased loaf pans or 1 large loaf pan. Bake at 350° for 40 to 45 minutes.

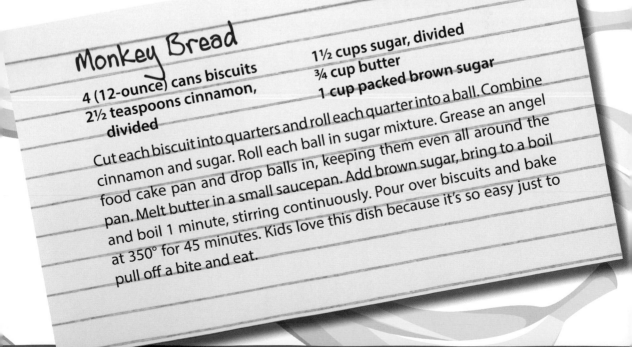

Monkey Bread

4 (12-ounce) cans biscuits
2½ teaspoons cinnamon, divided

1½ cups sugar, divided
¾ cup butter
1 cup packed brown sugar

Cut each biscuit into quarters and roll each quarter into a ball. Combine cinnamon and sugar. Roll each ball in sugar mixture. Grease an angel food cake pan and drop balls in, keeping them even all around the pan. Melt butter in a small saucepan. Add brown sugar, bring to a boil and boil 1 minute, stirring continuously. Pour over biscuits and bake at 350° for 45 minutes. Kids love this dish because it's so easy just to pull off a bite and eat.

Bread Teddy Bears

2 (1-pound) loaves frozen white
   bread dough, thawed according to
   package directions

1 egg
1 tablespoon water
16 raisins

Lightly grease 2 baking sheets. Cut each loaf of bread dough in half. Give each child 1 piece of dough and help them divide their piece into thirds. Shape 1 of the thirds into a ball for the bear's body and place 2 bodies on each baking sheet, leaving room for rest of bear. Have kids pinch off a little piece of dough from 1 of the remaining thirds to use for the muzzle later. Roll rest of that piece into a ball for the head. Place it next to the body on the baking sheet. To make paws and ears, divide remaining third of dough into 6 equal pieces. Roll each piece into a ball, then place 2 on each side of body for paws and 2 on top of the head for ears. Roll reserved piece of dough into a ball for the muzzle. Place muzzle on bottom of head. To connect bear parts, pinch dough pieces together. Cover bears with damp, clean kitchen towel. Let rise about 30 minutes or until almost double in size. Remove towel. Heat oven to 350°. In small bowl, beat egg with water. Gently brush bears with egg wash. Add 2 raisins for eyes, 1 raisin on muzzle for nose and 1 raisin for belly button. Bake 15 to 20 minutes until bread sounds hollow when tapped. Remove to wire racks and cool completely. Makes 4.

When did you get your first teddy bear?

_____

Does he have a name?
Who gave it to you?

_____

Name_____ Age_____

Pork and Bean Bread

1 cup raisins
1 cup boiling water
3 eggs
1 cup oil
2 cups sugar
1 (16-ounce) can pork and
    beans

2 cups flour
1 teaspoon cinnamon
1 teaspoon baking soda
½ teaspoon salt
½ teaspoon baking powder
1 cup chopped nuts
1 teaspoon vanilla

Mix raisins with boiling water. Stir and set aside. Beat eggs, oil, sugar and pork and beans until all beans are broken up. Add dry ingredients. Add nuts and vanilla. Drain raisins and add to mixture. Stir in well. Pour into 2 well-greased loaf pans. Bake at 325° for 50 to 60 minutes.

My favorite board game is:

_____

I like to play it with:

_____

Name_____ Age_____

Game Night Bread Sticks

Game night is for having fun with the family so heat up some soup and have the kids help you make these easy bread sticks to make it a special night.

1 (8-count) package hot dog buns
1 pound melted butter
Seasoning salt

Garlic salt
Parmesan cheese
Dried parsley

Cut each hot dog bun into 6 equal strips lengthwise (3 strips for top of bun; 3 for bottom). Dip strips in melted butter and place on cookie sheet, crowding strips together. Sprinkle with seasoning salt, garlic salt, Parmesan cheese and dried parsley to taste. Bake at 350° for 10 to 15 minutes or till lightly browned. Turn oven off and let set in oven several hours. Remove from oven and drain on paper towels. Store tightly covered; may be frozen. Great served with salads, soups and Italian food.

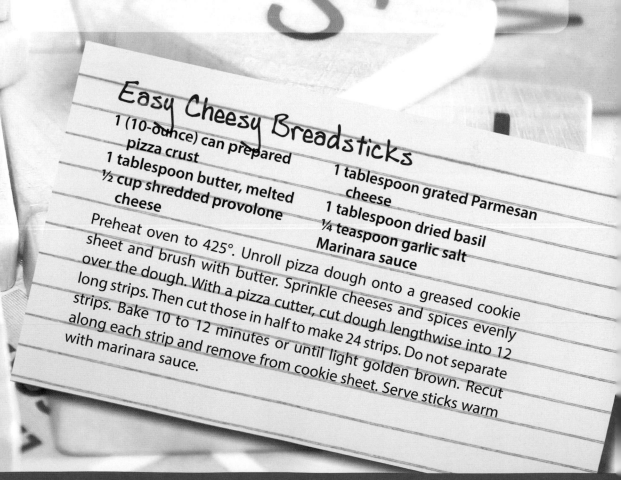

Easy Cheesy Breadsticks

1 (10-ounce) can prepared pizza crust
1 tablespoon butter, melted
½ cup shredded provolone cheese

1 tablespoon grated Parmesan cheese
1 tablespoon dried basil
¼ teaspoon garlic salt
Marinara sauce

Preheat oven to 425°. Unroll pizza dough onto a greased cookie sheet and brush with butter. Sprinkle cheeses and spices evenly over the dough. With a pizza cutter, cut dough lengthwise into 12 long strips. Then cut those in half to make 24 strips. Do not separate strips. Bake 10 to 12 minutes or until light golden brown. Recut along each strip and remove from cookie sheet. Serve sticks warm with marinara sauce.

Ice Cream Muffins

2 cups self-rising flour
1 pint vanilla ice cream, softened

Blend together flour and ice cream until well moistened. The batter will be lumpy. Fill 10 well-buttered muffin cups three-quarters full and bake at 350° for 20 minutes. Serves 5 to 10.

My favorite ice cream flavor:

☐ **Chocolate**   ☐ **Vanilla**   ☐ **Strawberry**

Name_____ Age_____

Strawberry Bread

1 (16-ounce) carton fresh
   strawberries
2¼ cups sugar, divided
1 teaspoon baking soda
1 teaspoon salt

1 teaspoon cinnamon
3 cups flour
4 eggs
1¼ cups oil
1½ cups chopped pecans

Top strawberries and slice into a bowl. Sprinkle ¼ cup sugar over strawberries and set aside. Sift together remaining 2 cups sugar with baking soda, salt, cinnamon and flour. Add strawberries, eggs and oil; mix well. Add pecans and divide dough between 2 (9x5-inch) treated loaf pans. Bake at 325° for 1 hour.

Triple Berry Breakfast Parfait

2 cups vanilla-flavored yogurt
¼ teaspoon ground cinnamon
1 cup sliced strawberries
½ cup blueberries

½ cup raspberries
1 cup low-fat granola without
   raisins

Combine yogurt and cinnamon in small bowl. Combine strawberries, blueberries and raspberries in medium bowl. For each parfait, layer ¼ cup fruit mixture, 2 tablespoons granola and ¼ cup yogurt mixture in 4 parfait glass. Repeat layers. Garnish with mint leaves, if desired. Makes 4 servings.

Tell me about your bedroom.

Color _____

I like my room because _____

_____

_____

Name _____ Age_____

Jelly-Cinnamon Toast

2 tablespoons soft butter
3 tablespoons currant jelly
½ teaspoon cinnamon
6 slices hot toast

Cream together butter, jelly and cinnamon. Spread lightly on 6 slices hot toast. Place under broiler 2 minutes or until jelly bubbles. Serves 6.

Sour Cream Rolls

1 cup self-rising flour
½ cup melted margarine
1 cup sour cream

Mix flour, margarine and sour cream. Pour into greased miniature muffin tins and bake at 450° for 15 minutes. Serves 4.

Toasted Faces

Milk
Food coloring
Bread

Pour milk into 3 or 4 glasses. Add enough food coloring to make milk brightly colored. Paint a face on bread slices with the colored milk. Toast in toaster.

What is your favorite subject in School?

_____

Teacher's Name:

_____

Name_____ Age_____

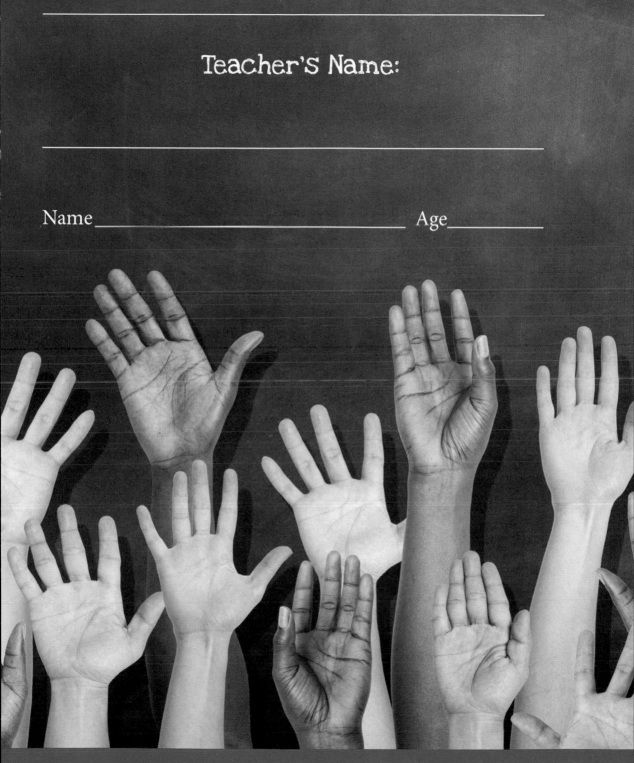

French Toast Sticks

8 thick slices bread (Texas Toast style or thick-cut French bread)
¼ cup melted butter
4 eggs
⅓ cup sugar
¼ teaspoon cinnamon
¾ teaspoon vanilla
⅔ cup milk

Preheat oven to 350°. Cut each slice of bread into 3 pieces to make sticks. In a bowl, mix together melted butter, eggs, sugar, cinnamon, vanilla and milk. Beat well. Dip sticks into egg mixture and place on a cookie sheet that has been sprayed with cooking spray. If there is any dip left, drizzle it over the sticks. Bake 25 minutes on middle rack of oven. Turn sticks halfway through baking time. Serve with syrup. To make ahead, allow sticks to cool. Flash freeze on cookie sheet, remove and place in a zip-close plastic bag. To reheat, place 3 sticks on a microwave-safe plate and heat on high 1 minute until warm.

Honey Bear French Toast

18 slices Texas toast-style bread or 1-inch-thick slices Italian bread
¼ cup all-purpose flour
1 tablespoon sugar
⅛ teaspoon salt
1 cup milk
3 eggs, lightly beaten
3 tablespoons butter
36 miniature chocolate chips
Warm honey

Using a 3½-inch, bear-shaped cookie cutter, cut bread into bear shapes. In a large bowl, whisk flour, sugar, salt, milk and eggs until smooth. Dip both sides of bread into egg mixture. In a large skillet, melt butter. Fry French toast for 2 to 3 minutes on each side or until golden brown. Transfer to serving plates; insert chocolate chips for eyes. Drizzle with honey. Makes 18 slices.

Fluffy Buttermilk Pancakes

This recipe makes the tastiest, fluffiest pancakes in the world.

2 cups all-purpose flour
1 teaspoon baking soda
2 teaspoons baking powder
3 to 4 tablespoons sugar
1 teaspoon salt

2 large eggs
1¾ cups buttermilk
½ cup sour cream
5 tablespoons melted butter
1 teaspoon vanilla, optional

In a large bowl, combine flour, baking soda, baking powder, sugar and salt. In another bowl whisk together eggs, buttermilk, sour cream, melted butter and vanilla. Add to the flour mixture and whisk until smooth (the batter will be thick). Let the mixture sit 5 minutes at room temperature. After 5 minutes whisk or mix again. Drop about ¼ cup batter onto a medium-hot skillet. Cook until lightly browned on the bottom, turn and cook until browned.

Oatmeal Pancakes

½ cup all-purpose flour
½ cup quick-cooking oats
¾ cup buttermilk
¼ cup milk
1 tablespoon sugar

2 tablespoons vegetable oil
1 teaspoon baking powder
½ teaspoon baking soda
½ teaspoon salt
1 egg

Beat all ingredients in a medium bowl with a hand beater until smooth. For thinner pancakes, stir in an additional 2 to 4 tablespoons milk. Using a pastry brush, grease a heated griddle, if necessary, with shortening. To test if griddle is just right. For each pancake, pour about ¼ cup batter onto the hot griddle. Cook until pancakes are puffed and dry around edges. Turn and cook other side until golden brown. Serve with applesauce if desired. Makes 10 to 12 pancakes.

Bunny Pancakes with Strawberry Butter

STRAWBERRY BUTTER:

1 (3-ounce) package cream
   cheese, softened
½ cup butter, softened

⅓ cup powdered sugar
1½ cups fresh or thawed frozen
   strawberries

Place cream cheese and butter in food processor or blender; process until smooth. Add powdered sugar; process until blended. Add strawberries and process until finely chopped.

BUNNY PANCAKES:

2 cups buttermilk baking
   mix
1 cup milk
2 eggs
½ cup plain yogurt
Assorted fruit and candies

Preheat electric skillet or griddle to 375°. Combine baking mix, milk, eggs and yogurt in medium bowl; mix well. Scoop up a scant cup of batter and with back of a spoon, gently spread batter into a 4-inch circle in heated skillet. Spoon 2 tablespoons batter onto top edge of circle for the head. Using back of spoon, spread batter from head to form bunny ears. Cook until bubbles on surface begin to pop and top of pancake starts to look dry. Carefully turn pancake over and cook until done, 1 to 2 minutes. Decorate with candies as desired. Repeat with remaining batter. Serve with Strawberry Butter. Makes about 12 (8-inch) pancakes.

what do you like to do
with your friends?

Name_____ Age_____

Wake-up Waffles

1 cup all-purpose flour
2 teaspoons baking powder
1 teaspoon sugar
¼ teaspoon salt
1 cup milk
¼ cup margarine or butter, melted
1 egg, separated

Heat waffle iron. Mix flour, baking powder, sugar and salt in a medium bowl. Stir in milk, margarine and egg yolk until blended. Beat egg white in a small bowl on high speed until stiff peaks form; fold flour mixture into egg white. Pour about ⅔ cup batter onto center of the hot waffle iron and cook until golden. Makes 3 (8-inch) waffles.

Chocolate Chip Waffles

1 package Chocolate Chip Muffin Mix
¾ cup all-purpose flour
1 teaspoon baking powder
1¾ cups milk
2 eggs
5 tablespoons butter or margarine, melted
Powdered sugar, optional

Preheat and lightly grease waffle iron according to manufacturer's directions. Combine muffin mix, flour and baking powder in large bowl. Add milk, eggs and melted butter. Stir until moistened, about 50 strokes. Pour batter onto center grids of preheated waffle iron. Bake according to manufacturer's directions until golden brown. Remove baked waffle carefully with fork. Repeat with remaining batter. Dust lightly with powdered sugar and top with fresh fruit, syrup, grated chocolate or whipped cream, if desired. Makes 10 to 12 waffles.

What is your favorite memory from camp or a camping trip?

_____

_____

Name_____ Age_____

Sunny Day Breakfast Burrito

1 tablespoon butter
½ cup chopped red bell pepper
2 green onions, sliced
6 eggs
2 tablespoons milk

¼ teaspoon salt
4 (7-inch) flour tortillas, warmed
½ cup shredded Mexican blend
    cheese
½ cup salsa

Melt butter in medium skillet over medium heat. Add bell pepper and green onions; cook and stir about 3 minutes or until tender. Beat eggs, milk and salt in medium bowl. Add egg mixture to skillet; reduce heat to low. Cook, stirring gently, until eggs are just set. They should be soft with no liquid remaining. Spoon egg mixture down center of tortillas; top with cheese. Fold in sides and roll to enclose filling. Serve with salsa. Makes 4 servings.

Sausage, Egg and Biscuit Casserole

1 (12-ounce) can buttermilk biscuits
1 pound pork sausage
6 eggs
¾ cup milk
Salt and pepper to taste
1 cup shredded mozzarella cheese
1 cup shredded Cheddar cheese

Cut biscuits into 6 to 8 pieces and place in greased 8x8-inch pan. Brown sausage in a skillet, drain and spread over biscuits. Beat eggs; mix with milk, salt and pepper. Pour over sausage and biscuits. Sprinkle both cheeses over top and bake at 425° for 30 to 35 minutes. Let sit 5 minutes before serving.

Scrambled Eggs

6 eggs
¼ cup milk
¼ teaspoon salt
¼ teaspoon pepper
3 tablespoons margarine

Break eggs into small mixing bowl being careful not to get any eggshell in the eggs. Add milk, salt and pepper. Beat mixture with fork. Place margarine in skillet; heat over medium heat until margarine is melted. Pour egg mixture into skillet. Scramble with fork or spatula until eggs look fairly dry.

Egg Carton Planter

1 cardboard egg carton
Tray to hold the egg carton
Potting soil
Water
Seeds (flower, herb or vegetable)
Plastic wrap

Cut an egg carton in half lengthwise along the fold between the top and bottom. Poke a hole from the inside out in the center of each egg cup to allow water to drain. Place egg carton in tray to prevent water from making a mess. Fill each cup with potting soil. Pour a little water slowly into each cup. Drop a few seeds into each cup and cover with soil. Label seeds if using more than 1 kind. Cover tray with plastic wrap. Poke a few holes in plastic to let air in. Place tray in a sunny spot. Remove plastic when seeds sprout. Water as needed. Clip off smaller sprouts in each cup so that only 1 plant is growing in each. When large enough, seedlings may be planted in yard or garden.

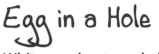 Egg in a Hole

**White or wheat sandwich
  bread**
Vegetable oil

Eggs
Salt and pepper

Use a glass to cut center out of a slice of bread. Heat oil in skillet. Place bread in skillet. Break egg carefully so that contents fall into the hole. Salt and pepper to taste. Fry until egg is cooked through. May need to turn. Repeat for more sandwiches.

Have you ever made a hole-in-one?

☐ Yes
☐ No

Name_____ Age_____

Flubber

Kids love this stuff and it's even fun for adults!

2 cups white glue
1½ cups warm water
Blue food coloring
Yellow food coloring
3 teaspoons borax
1 cup hot water

Combine glue and warm water; add blue and yellow food color to reach a "flubber" green. In a separate bowl, dissolve borax in hot water. Add to glue mixture one third at a time, mixing thoroughly with hands after each addition. After some kneading the product will bind together into flubber. From there, give it to a kid and they will know exactly what to do with it. Super easy yet super fun.

Vegetable Soup

1 (46-ounce) can V-8 juice
1 (20-ounce) package frozen mixed
    vegetables
1 (2-ounce) package onion soup

Combine ingredients in a large saucepan; stir and heat until mixture comes to a boil. Reduce heat and simmer 20 minutes, stirring often. Season to taste. Great with cornbread! Serves 6 to 8.

Easy Slow Cooker Potato Soup

1 (30-ounce) bag frozen, shredded hash browns
3 (14-ounce) cans chicken broth
1 (10.75-ounce) can cream of chicken soup
½ cup chopped onion
¼ teaspoon ground pepper
1 (8-ounce) package cream cheese
Bacon, shredded Cheddar cheese, green onion, sour cream
    for garnish

Combine everything except cream cheese and garnish items in slow Cooker. Cook on low 6 to 8 hours. About an hour before serving, add cream cheese and cook until thoroughly melted. Ladle soup into bowls and top with bacon, Cheddar cheese, green onion and/or sour cream.

Dotted Soup

3 wieners
1 (10.75-ounce) can tomato soup
1 soup can milk
Parmesan cheese

Cut wieners crosswise into thin circles. Pour soup into saucepan. Slowly add the milk, stirring until mixture is smooth. Stir and cook over medium heat until mixture is hot. Do not boil. Add wiener slices to soup. Cook over medium heat 5 minutes more. Do not boil. Pour soup into bowls and sprinkle with Parmesan cheese.

Taco Soup

1 pound ground beef
1 onion, diced
3 cups water
1 quart stewed tomatoes
2 (15-ounce) cans kidney beans
1 (8-ounce) can tomato sauce
1 (1.25-ounce) envelope taco seasoning

Brown ground beef and onions; drain fat. Add remaining ingredients. Cook 15 minutes. Serve with shredded cheese, crushed corn chips and a dab of sour cream.

What is your favorite thing to wear?

_____

What color is it?

_____

Why is it your favorite?

_____

Name_____ Age_____

What is your favorite summer memory?

_____

_____

Name_____

Age _____

Carrot Raisin Salad

2 carrots, peeled   **4 tablespoons mayonnaise**
½ cup raisins

Shred carrots using grater. Combine with raisins and mayonnaise. Serve immediately.

Dried Apple Ornaments

1 apple
2 cups lemon juice
1 tablespoon salt
Shellac
Paintbrush
Ribbon

Begin by polishing your apple with a soft cloth. Slice the apple in round slices beginning at the top and slicing to bottom. Slice completely through the apple core to retain the pretty design in the center. You'll probably get 4 good slices from the apple, as the top and bottom slices are to be discarded (or eaten). Combine lemon juice and salt; soak apple slices 3 minutes. Drain, and then poke a hole near the top of each slice. Bake 6 hours at 150°. Let cool. Shellac 1 side and allow to dry. Flip and shellac other side. When dry, thread a pretty ribbon through hole and hang.

Tomato Flower

Lettuce leaves
4 tomatoes
Cottage cheese
Paprika
French dressing

Rinse and drain lettuce. Cut out core of tomatoes to hollow them out and then cut each tomato into 8 wedges, being careful not to cut all the way through. Place on lettuce leaves. Fill tomatoes with cottage cheese. Sprinkle with paprika. Pour French dressing over top.

5-Cup Salad

1 cup pineapple chunks
1 cup mandarin orange segments
1 cup shredded coconut
1 cup miniature marshmallows
1 cup sour cream

Mix all ingredients together and chill.

Have you ever flown a kite?

☐ Yes   ☐ No

Make this kite your favorite color!

What is your favorite color?

Name_____ Age_____

Red Applesauce Salad

1 (16-ounce) jar applesauce
1 (3-ounce) package cherry Jell-O
¾ cup 7-Up

Place applesauce in small saucepan; heat over medium heat until bubbly hot. Add Jell-O and stir until dissolved. Cool. Stir in 7-Up; mix well. Pour into mold. Chill until set. Makes 8 to 10 servings.

Frozen Grapes

Pick seedless grapes off bunch and place on dish. Freeze. Eat like candy!

Funny Bunny Salad

Pear halves
Raisins
Cherries
Marshmallows
Almonds

Arrange ingredients on a platter, using the pear halves for the body, raisins for eyes, cherries for the nose and mouth, marshmallows for the tail and almonds for ears.

Green Grape Salad

¼ cup mayonnaise
1 (3-ounce) package cream cheese, softened
Pinch garlic salt
1 pound seedless green grapes

Combine mayonnaise and cream cheese; beat until smooth. Add garlic salt; beat again. Add grapes and stir until grapes are coated. Chill until serving time. Makes 4 to 6 servings.

SUPER

Who is your favorite super hero?

_____

Name_____ Age_____

Peanut Butter & Jelly Open-Faced Super Hero Sandwiches

This fun sandwich will give your super hero the energy they need to save the world.

1 English muffin
2 tablespoons creamy peanut butter
2 tablespoons strawberry jam
6 to 8 slices banana
Chocolate syrup
Sweetened flaked coconut, optional

Split and toast English muffin. Spread peanut butter on cut sides of English muffin. Spread jam over peanut butter. Top with banana slices. Drizzle with chocolate syrup to taste. Sprinkle with coconut flakes if desired. Serve warm.

Sport Sandwiches

⅓ cup peanut butter
¼ cup cream cheese, softened
2 tablespoons honey
Bread

Place peanut butter, cream cheese and honey in mixing bowl. Stir until well blended. Trim crusts from bread. Use a round cookie cutter to make ball shapes. Spread peanut butter mixture on half the balls and top with remaining balls. May be covered and refrigerated until ready to serve.

Circle your favorite Sport.

Name_____ Age_____

Inside-Out Turkey Sandwiches

You'll find the bread on the inside of this tasty snack.

2 tablespoons cream cheese, softened
2 tablespoons pasteurized process cheese spread
2 teaspoons chopped green onion tops
1 teaspoon prepared mustard
12 thin, round slices fat-free turkey breast or smoked turkey breast
4 large pretzel logs or unsalted bread sticks

Combine cream cheese, process cheese spread, green onion and mustard in small bowl; mix well. Arrange 3 turkey slices on large sheet of plastic wrap, overlapping slices in center. Spread one fourth of cream cheese mixture evenly onto turkey slices, covering slices completely. Place 1 pretzel at bottom edge of turkey slices; roll up turkey around pretzel. (Be sure to keep all 3 turkey slices together as you roll them around pretzel.) Repeat with remaining ingredients. Makes 4 servings.

Banana Berry Peanut Pitas

1 (8-ounce) package small pita breads, cut crosswise in halves
16 teaspoons peanut butter
16 teaspoons strawberry spreadable fruit
1 large banana, peeled and thinly sliced (about 48 slices)

Spread inside of each pita half with 1 teaspoon each peanut butter and spreadable fruit. Fill pita halves evenly with banana slices. Serve immediately. Makes 8 servings.

Variations: Honey Bees: Substitute honey for spreadable fruit. Jolly Jellies: Substitute any flavor jelly for spreadable fruit and thin apple slices for banana slices. P.B. Crunchers: Substitute reduced fat mayonnaise for spreadable fruit and celery slices for banana slices.

Cheese Delight Sandwich

1 slice bread	1 slice tomato
Mayonnaise	1 slice onion
1 slice cheese	1 strip bacon

Spread bread with mayonnaise. Add in layers, cheese, tomato and onion. Cut bacon strip in half and place on onion. Place sandwich on broiler pan. Turn oven setting to broil and broil until cheese begins to melt.

Cheese Puff Sandwiches

8 slices bread

4 slices Cheddar cheese

2 eggs

1 cup milk

½ teaspoon salt

Pinch pepper

¼ teaspoon dry mustard

Preheat oven to 350°. Arrange 4 bread slices in large greased baking dish. Cover each with a cheese slice. Place remaining bread slices on cheese slices. Beat eggs until frothy. Add milk, salt, pepper and dry mustard: Mix well. Pour over sandwiches. Refrigerate until milk is absorbed into bread. Bake at 350° for 30 minutes. Makes 4 servings.

Funny Face Sandwich Melts

2 super-size English muffins, split and toasted

8 teaspoons French's Sweet & Tangy Honey Mustard

1 (8-ounce) can crushed pineapple, drained

8 ounces sliced smoked ham

4 slices Swiss or white American cheese

Preferred topping for making funny faces: carrots, cucumber, lettuce, olives, pickles, tomatoes, etc

Place English muffins, cut side up, on baking sheet. Spread each with 2 teaspoons mustard. Arrange one fourth of the pineapple, ham and cheese on top of each muffin. Broil until cheese melts, about 1 minute. Decorate with additional mustard and assorted vegetables to create your own funny face. Makes 4 servings.

Who was your first boyfriend/ girlfriend?

_____

Name_____

Age _____

Have a Heart Sandwich

Heart-shaped cookie cutter
Whole-wheat bread slices
White bread slices
Strawberries
Softened cream cheese

Using cookie cutter, cut hearts out of bread. Wash berries, core and chop most of them, leaving a few whole. Mix chopped berries with cream cheese. Spread on a white heart. Top with a wheat heart. Serve 2 hearts to each guest with a few whole strawberries for garnish.

play dough

1 cup flour
½ cup salt
1 tablespoon cream of tartar

1 cup water
1 tablespoon vegetable oil
8 or 9 drops food coloring

Sift together flour, salt and cream of tartar. Boil water, oil and food coloring, Pour over flour mixture and mix together. When cool enough to handle, knead a few times. Store in plastic zip-close bag when not in use.

Twice Baked Potatoes

3 hot baked potatoes, split lengthwise
½ cup sour cream
2 tablespoons butter or margarine
1⅓ cups French's French Fried Onions, divided
2 cups shredded Cheddar cheese, divided
Dash paprika, optional

Preheat oven to 400°. Scoop out insides of potatoes into medium bowl, leaving thin shells. Mash potatoes with sour cream and butter until smooth. Stir in 1 cup French Fried Onions and 1 cup cheese. Spoon mixture into shells. Bake 20 minutes or until heated through. Top with remaining onions, cheese and paprika, if desired. Bake 2 minutes or until cheese melts. Makes 6 servings.

Tip: To bake potatoes quickly, microwave on high 10 to 12 minutes until tender.

Bacon Ranch Foil-Packet Potatoes

10 to 12 baby red potatoes, thinly sliced
6 slices cooked and crumbled bacon
1 red onion, thin sliced (optional)
1 (1-ounce) packet ranch dressing mix
Salt and pepper to taste
3 tablespoons butter
Sour cream, optional

Spray 3 sheets heavy-duty foil with cooking spray. Top each piece with equal portions of potatoes, bacon, onions and ranch dressing mix. Add salt and pepper to taste. Add 1 tablespoon butter to each packet. Wrap securely. Grill 20 to 30 minutes. Let stand 10 minutes before serving. Serve in foil, topped with sour cream if desired.

Homemade Potato Chips

2 unpeeled potatoes, scrubbed
Vegetable oil
Salt or garlic salt

Add ½ inch of oil to a skillet and heat. Slice potatoes very thinly and fry in hot oil until crisp and golden brown. Drain and sprinkle with salt.

Slow Cooker Potatoes

8 to medium potatoes, peeled and diced
1 stick margarine
1 (8-ounce) container sour cream
2 (10.75 ounce) cans Cheddar cheese soup
Instant onions to taste

Boil potatoes in salted water to cover until almost done; drain. Melt margarine in a slow cooker set to high. Add sour cream and soup; mix well. Add potatoes and mix. Cover slow cooker, set to low, and cook potatoes 1 hour. This is a simple recipe that tastes great.

Sliced Baked Potato

This recipe is even better than fries.

Potatoes	**Sea salt**
Olive oil	**Pepper**
Melted butter	

Cut potatoes into slices being careful not to go all the way through. Place on pieces of foil or ovenproof dish. Drizzle olive oil and butter over the slices and sprinkle tops with sea salt and pepper. Bake at 425° for 40 minutes.

What is your favorite book?

_____

Name_____ Age_____

Do you like to read?

◻ **Yes** ◻ **No**

Veggie Bites

⅓ cup melted margarine or butter, divided

1 egg

2 teaspoons water

½ cup all-purpose flour

½ teaspoon salt

2 cups fresh vegetables (broccoli or cauliflower florets, ¼-inch carrot slices,
  ½-inch zucchini slices, ½-inch strips green or red pepper)

Grated Parmesan cheese, optional

Heat oven to 450°. Place 1 tablespoon margarine in a 9x13-inch baking dish in oven to melt. Beat egg and water with a fork in a shallow dish. Mix flour and salt in another shallow dish. Dip about ¼ cup vegetables into egg mixture. Remove 1 piece at time with a slotted spoon, fork or hands; roll in flour mixture to coat. Place in prepared pan. Repeat with remaining vegetables. Carefully pour remaining margarine over each vegetable piece and into pan. Bake, uncovered, turning once, until vegetables are crisp-tender and coating is golden brown, 10 to 12 minutes. Drain. Sprinkle lightly with Parmesan cheese if you like.

How do you wear your hair?

☐ **Long**   ☐ **Short**

☐ **The way my Mom makes me.**

What color is your hair?

If you could wear it anyway you wanted, how would you cut your hair?

Name _____

Age _____

Zucchini Parmesan Crisps

1 pound zucchini or summer squash, about 2 medium-sized
1 tablespoon olive oil
⅓ cup panko breadcrumbs
⅓ cup shredded Parmesan
¼ teaspoon kosher salt
Freshly ground pepper to taste

Preheat oven to 400°. Line 2 baking sheets with foil and spray lightly with vegetable spray. Slice zucchini or squash into ¼-inch-thick rounds. Toss with oil, coating well. In a wide bowl or plate, combine breadcrumbs, Parmesan, salt and pepper. Place rounds in Parmesan-breadcrumb mixture, pressing lightly to adhere and turning so there is a light coating on both sides. Place rounds in a single layer on baking sheets. Sprinkle any remaining breadcrumb mixture over the rounds. Bake 22 to 27 minutes until golden brown. (There is no need to flip them during baking—they crisp up on both sides as is.)

Microwave Glazed Sweet Potatoes

4 medium sweet potatoes
½ cup firmly packed brown sugar
¼ cup margarine

Pierce sweet potatoes with a fork. Place in microwave oven. (Important: Never put metal or aluminum foil in the microwave oven.) Microwave on high 10 minutes or until tender. Peel and slice into 1½ quart glass baking dish. Sprinkle potato slices with brown sugar. Dot with margarine. Cover with glass lid or plastic wrap. Microwave on high 4 minutes; stir. Microwave on high 3 minutes longer. Let stand, covered, 3 minutes before serving.

Yam-Pineapple Bake

4 cups cooked or canned yams or sweet potatoes, peeled and mashed
1 (8-ounce) can pineapple tidbits with syrup
3 tablespoons softened butter
1 teaspoon salt
16 marshmallows, divided
¼ cup pecan halves

Combine yams or sweet potatoes, pineapple tidbits with syrup, butter and salt. Place half the mixture in buttered 2-quart casserole. Top with 8 marshmallows. Add remaining yam mixture. Top with pecan halves. Cover casserole and bake at 350° for 30 minutes. Top with remaining marshmallows. Bake, uncovered, 10 minutes more. Serves 6.

What food do you not like?

_____

Name _____

Age _____

Check the foods you like:

☐ **Broccoli** ☐ **Chicken**
☐ **Pizza** ☐ **Beets**
☐ **Oranges** ☐ **Sauerkraut**
☐ **Cheese** ☐ **Ice Cream**
☐ **Pickles** ☐ **Spaghetti**

Fresh Broccoli with Mild Cheese Sauce

1 bunch broccoli
1 teaspoon salt
Pinch pepper
2 tablespoons butter or margarine
2 tablespoons flour
1 cup milk
1 cup shredded American cheese

Rinse broccoli; remove large leaves and tough part of stalks. Separate into individual spears. Place in large saucepan with ½ inch boiling water. Add salt and pepper. Simmer 10 to 12 minutes or until tender-crisp. Drain and keep warm. Melt butter in a saucepan. Stir in flour until smooth. Add milk, stirring constantly. Cook until sauce thickens and comes to a boil. Add cheese. Cook, stirring, until melted and blended. Cover broccoli with cheese sauce. Makes 4 to 6 servings.

What is your favorite video game?

_____

Who do you play
video games with?

_____

SELECT YOUR CHARACTER

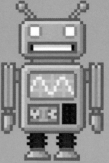

I mostly play video games:
- [ ] in my bedroom
- [ ] in the living room
- [ ] at a friend's house
- [ ] somewhere else
- [ ] not at all

Fried Cabbage Dish

1 pound bacon, finely chopped
1 medium onion, chopped
2 pounds cabbage, finely diced
¼ teaspoon red pepper flakes
½ teaspoon salt
½ teaspoon black pepper

Fry bacon until crisp and well browned. Drain and set aside. Add chopped onion to the bacon grease and cook, stirring, until translucent. Add cabbage, pepper flakes, salt and pepper, stirring until all cabbage is coated. Add the crumbled bacon. Cover and cook over low heat until cabbage is tender.

Candied Carrots

¼ cup margarine
¼ cup jellied cranberry sauce
2 tablespoons sugar
½ teaspoon salt
4 cups canned sliced carrots

Preheat oven to 350°. Combine margarine, cranberry sauce, sugar and salt in skillet. Simmer on low heat until cranberry sauce melts, stirring often. Drain carrots and add to cranberry mixture, stirring well. Place in baking dish. Bake 10 minutes.

Can you help the rabbits find something to eat?

What foods do rabbits like?

Confetti Corn

2 eggs
3 tablespoons margarine
2 (15-ounce) cans whole-kernel corn
1 (4-ounce) jar chopped pimento, drained
1 teaspoon salt
¼ teaspoon pepper
1 (3-ounce) can onion rings

Preheat oven to 350°. Grease 1½-quart baking dish. Break eggs into mixing bowl; beat well. Heat margarine in small saucepan over low heat until melted. Combine eggs, margarine, corn, pimento, salt and pepper in baking dish; mix well. Top with onion rings. Bake at 350° for 35 minutes.

Creamy Corn

¼ cup milk
1 (3-ounce) package cream cheese
1 tablespoon margarine
½ teaspoon salt
Pinch pepper
3 cups whole-kernel corn

Combine milk, cream cheese, margarine, salt and pepper in large saucepan. Cook over low heat, stirring constantly, until blended. Drain corn well. Stir into cream cheese mixture and heat through.

Loaded Cauliflower

1 cup cooked cauliflower

1 teaspoon butter, melted

Salt and pepper to taste

2 tablespoons shredded
   Cheddar cheese

1 tablespoon ranch dressing or
   sour cream

1 strip bacon, cooked and
   crumbled

1 teaspoon chives

Place cauliflower in a small baking dish. Top with melted butter and season with salt and pepper. Top with cheese. Microwave or broil until cheese is melted. Top with ranch dressing, bacon and chives.

Do you pray at bedtime?
☐ **Yes** ☐ **No**

Name_____ Age_____

Microwave Honeyed Onions

8 pearl onions, peeled
2 tablespoons margarine
½ cup honey

Place onions in 1-quart glass baking dish. Cover with glass lid or plastic wrap. Microwave on high 8 minutes; drain. Stir in margarine and honey; cover. Microwave on high 3 minutes longer. Let stand, covered, 3 minutes before serving.

When do you read the Bible?

☐ in the morning

☐ at Sunday School

☐ at night

☐ I don't

What is your favorite hobby?

_____

Name_____

Age _____

No-Fuss Lasagna

1 (28-ounce) jar pasta sauce
6 uncooked lasagna noodles
1 (15-ounce) container ricotta cheese
2 cups (8 ounces) shredded mozzarella cheese or pizza cheese blend, divided
⅓ cup grated Parmesan cheese

Preheat oven to 375°. Spread 1 cup pasta sauce in an 11x7-inch baking dish. Arrange 3 uncooked noodles over sauce; top with ricotta cheese, 1 cup mozzarella cheese, Parmesan cheese and 1 cup pasta sauce. Top with remaining 3 uncooked noodles and remaining pasta sauce. Cover and bake 55 minutes. Uncover and top with remaining mozzarella cheese. Bake 5 minutes more or until cheese is melted. Let stand 10 minutes before cutting. Makes 6 servings.

Yummiest Ever Baked Mac and Cheese

1 pound elbow macaroni, cooked al dente
2 (10.75-ounce) cans Cheddar cheese soup
2 (12-ounce) cans evaporated milk
1¼ sticks butter
1 teaspoon salt
1 teaspoon pepper
6 cups shredded Cheddar cheese

Preheat oven to 350°. Drain macaroni and set aside. Combine soup, evaporated milk, butter, salt and pepper in a saucepan and cook until butter is melted (can also be heated in the microwave). Spread a third of cooked noodles in a 9x13-inch baking dish. Top with a third of the sauce. Sprinkle with a third of the Cheddar cheese. Repeat layers twice, ending with cheese. Bake 40 to 45 minutes. Let stand 5 minutes before serving.

Mexican Tortilla Stacks

1 tablespoon vegetable oil
½ cup chopped onion
1 (15-ounce) can black beans, drained and rinsed
1 (14.5-ounce) can Mexican or Italian-style diced tomatoes
1 cup frozen corn
1 (1¼-ounce) envelope taco seasoning mix
6 (6-inch) corn tortillas
2 cups shredded Cheddar cheese
1 cup water
Sour cream, optional
Sliced black olives, optional

Preheat oven to 350°. Spray a 9x13-inch baking dish with nonstick cooking spray. Heat oil in large skillet over medium-high heat until hot. Add onion; cook and stir 3 minutes or until tender. Add beans, tomatoes with juice, corn and taco seasoning mix. Bring to a boil over high heat. Reduce heat to low and simmer 5 minutes. Place 2 tortillas side by side in prepared dish. Top each tortilla with about ½ cup bean mixture. Sprinkle evenly with cheese. Repeat layers twice, creating 2 tortilla stacks each 3 tortillas high. Pour water around sides of tortillas. Cover tightly with foil and bake 30 to 35 minutes or until heated through. Cut into wedges; serve with sour cream and black olives, if desired. Makes 6 servings.

Cowboy Beans

2 (15-ounce) cans pork and beans
⅓ cup firmly packed brown sugar
1 small onion, finely chopped
¼ cup ketchup
5 slices bacon

Preheat oven to 350°. Pour pork and beans into 1½-quart casserole. Add brown sugar, onion and ketchup; mix well. Top with bacon slices. Bake at 350° for 1 hour.

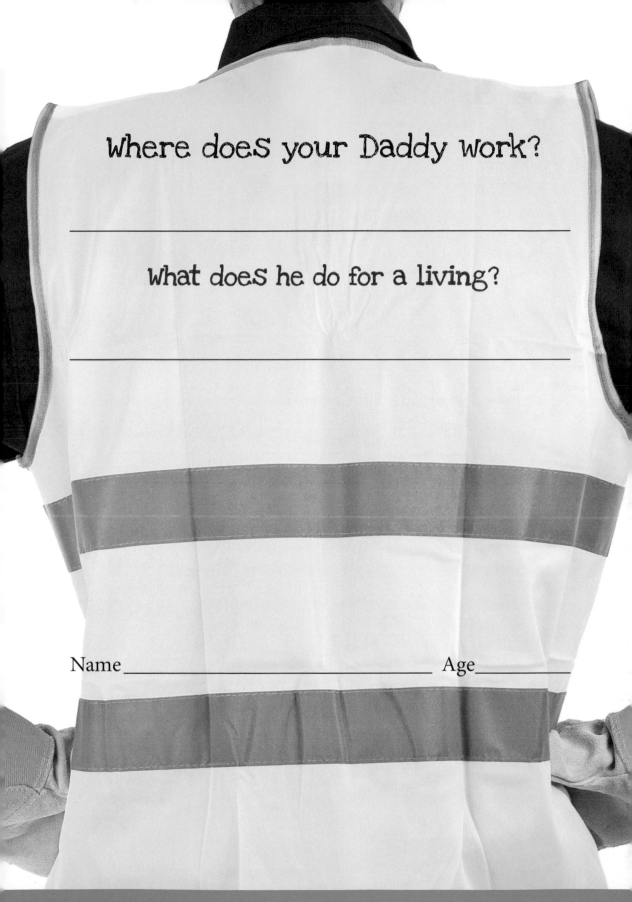

Honey-Butter Peas

1 (12-ounce) package frozen
   green peas
¼ cup honey
¼ cup margarine, softened

Prepare peas according to package directions; drain. Combine honey and margarine in small mixer bowl; beat until fluffy. Pour over peas. Serve immediately.

Do you like peas?

☐ Yes

☐ No

☐ Are you kidding?

Asparagus Bake

1 (15-ounce) can asparagus

3 slices American cheese

1 (10.75-ounce) can cream of mushroom soup

Preheat oven to 350°. Drain asparagus and place in a 2-quart baking dish. Break cheese into small pieces; add to asparagus. Pour soup over asparagus mixture. Bake 30 minutes.

Delicious Green Beans

2 (15-ounce) cans green beans

1 (10.75-ounce) can cream of celery soup

Preheat oven to 425°. Drain liquid from green beans, reserving ½ cup liquid. Mix liquid with soup. Arrange green beans in baking dish. Pour soup mixture over beans. Cover and bake at 425° for 45 minutes.

Balloon Creations

Plaster of Paris
Balloons, medium-size
Funnel with large opening
Paint or decorations

Mix 2 cups plaster of Paris with 1 cup water until creamy. Blow up a balloon then deflate it. Pour plaster into empty balloon using funnel; tie balloon. Begin to mold the balloon into your desired shape. As the plaster of Paris hardens, the balloon will hold any shape you mold it into. Once plaster is set enough to hold the shape, place balloon on table and allow to dry at least a half hour. Tear off balloon and decorate as desired.

Sloppy Joes

1 pound ground beef

1 teaspoon salt

½ cup ketchup

2 tablespoons mustard

2 tablespoons
   Worcestershire
   sauce

Few drops liquid
   smoke

2 tablespoons brown
   sugar

Brown ground beef and salt; add
remaining ingredients and simmer a few
minutes before serving.

Who is your favorite princess?

_____

Name_____ Age_____

If I lived in a castle, I would:

_____

_____

Copycat White Castle Burgers

1½ pounds ground beef
1 (2-ounce) package Lipton onion soup mix
1 tablespoon peanut butter
½ cup milk
1 onion, finely diced
Cheese slices
Sara Lee Classic Dinner Rolls, sliced in half

In a large bowl, mix ground beef, onion soup mix, peanut butter and milk. Spread mixture on a cookie sheet. Use a rolling pin to roll over meat to smooth it out. Bake at 350° for 10 minutes. Remove from oven. Meat will have shrunk in the oven; spread diced onions around edges where the pan is showing. Bake another 15 minutes. Remove from oven and spoon onions from edges over top of meat. Distribute cheese slices over meat. Return to oven until cheese melts, 5 to 10 minutes. Distribute tops of rolls over meat; return to oven 5 more minutes. Remove from oven. Slice with a pizza cutter; pick up meat and top buns with a spatula and set on bottom buns.

Hamburgers

1 pound ground beef (chuck or round steak)
¾ teaspoon salt
1 tablespoon ice water
1 tablespoon butter

Mix ground beef, salt and ice water together lightly and quickly and shape into 4 patties. Melt butter in large frying pan. When hot, add hamburgers and cook over high heat until browned on 1 side. Turn and brown on other side. Reduce heat and cook 3 to 5 minutes on each side, to desired doneness. Serves 4.

What toppings do you like?

☐ Cheese   ☐ Ketchup

☐ Mustard   ☐ Mayo

☐ Lettuce   ☐ Onion

☐ Tomato   ☐ Pickles

Quick Cheeseburger Pie

CRUST:

⅓ cup all-purpose flour

½ teaspoon salt

½ cup shortening

3 to 4 tablespoons cold water

FILLING:

1 pound ground beef

½ to ¾ cup finely chopped onion

1 clove garlic, finely chopped

½ teaspoon salt

¼ cup all-purpose flour

⅓ cup dill pickle liquid

⅓ cup milk

½ cup chopped dill pickles

2 cups shredded American or Swiss
    cheese, divided

Heat oven to 425°. Prepare pastry by mixing flour and salt together in a bowl. Cut in shortening with a pastry blender until mixture looks like tiny peas. Sprinkle in cold water 1 tablespoon at a time, stirring with a fork after each addition. Mix lightly until all flour is moistened and pastry almost cleans sides of bowl. Add 1 to 2 teaspoons more water if necessary. Pat in bottom and up sides of 8x2-inch quiche dish or 8x1½-inch round pan. Bake 15 minutes.

Cook and stir beef, onion and garlic in 10-inch skillet until brown; drain. Sprinkle with salt and flour. Stir in pickle liquid, milk, pickles and 1 cup cheese. Spoon into dish. Bake 15 minutes; sprinkle with remaining cheese. Bake until crust is golden brown, about 5 minutes longer. Makes 4 to 6 servings.

Hamburger Pie

2 pounds ground beef

Salt and pepper to taste

2 teaspoons chopped onion

1 (32-ounce) package frozen shoestring French fries

1 (10.75-ounce) can cream of chicken soup

1 (10.75-ounce) can cream of mushroom soup

Preheat oven to 350°. Pat ground beef into bottom of a 9x13-inch pan to make a crust. Sprinkle with salt, pepper and onion. Arrange frozen French fries over hamburger. Spread soups over French fries. Bake 1 hour. Cut into squares to serve. Makes 8 servings.

What school award have you won?

_____

Name_____

Age _____

Individual Meatloaves

1 egg, beaten
⅓ cup breadcrumbs
¼ cup milk
2 tablespoons ketchup

½ pound ground beef
½ teaspoon onion salt
Dash black pepper

Preheat oven to 350°. Beat egg, breadcrumbs, milk and ketchup in mixing bowl. Add beef, onion salt and pepper; mix with fork or hands. Fill 6 muffin cups two-thirds full. Bake 30 minutes. (To bake in one loaf, increase baking time to 45 minutes.)

Kid's Choice Award-Winning Meatballs

1½ pounds ground beef
¼ cup dry seasoned breadcrumbs
3 tablespoons Worcestershire sauce

¼ cup grated Parmesan cheese
1 egg
2 (14-ounce) jars spaghetti sauce

Preheat oven to 425°. In bowl, gently mix beef, breadcrumbs, Worcestershire, cheese and egg. Shape into 1-inch meatballs. Place meatballs on rack in roasting pan. Bake 15 minutes or until cooked through. In large saucepan, combine meatballs and spaghetti sauce. Cook until heated through. Serve over cooked pasta. Makes 6 to 8 servings (about 48 meatballs).

Quick Meatball Tip: On wax paper, pat meat mixture into 8x6x1-inch rectangle. With knife, cut crosswise and lengthwise into 1-inch rows. Roll each small square into a ball.

Porcupine Meatballs

1 pound ground beef
¼ cup long-grain rice, uncooked
1 egg, slightly beaten
1 tablespoon chopped fresh parsley (or ½ tablespoon dried parsley)
2 tablespoons finely chopped onion
½ teaspoon salt
Dash black pepper
1 (10.5-ounce) can tomato soup, divided
½ cup water
1 teaspoon Worcestershire sauce

Combine ground beef, rice, egg, parsley, onion, salt, pepper and ¼ cup tomato soup. Mix well. Shape mixture into about 20 small meatballs. Place meatballs in a large skillet. Mix rest of soup, water and Worcestershire in a small bowl; pour over meatballs. Bring to a boil. Reduce heat, cover, and simmer 40 minutes or until meatballs are cooked and rice is soft, stirring often.

What do you think is gross?

_____

_____

Name_____ Age_____

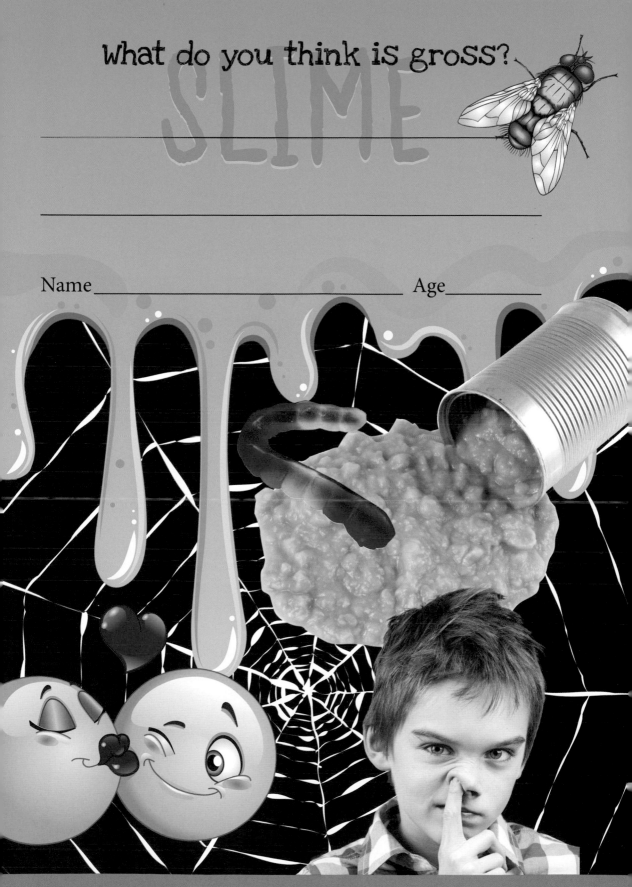

Pizza Rollers

1 (13.8-ounce) package refrigerated pizza dough
½ cup pizza sauce
18 slices pepperoni
6 sticks mozzarella cheese

Preheat oven to 425°. Coat baking sheet with nonstick cooking spray. Roll out pizza dough on baking sheet to form 12x9-inch rectangle. Cut pizza dough into 6 rectangles. Spread about 1 tablespoon sauce over center third of each rectangle. Top with 3 slices pepperoni and a stick of mozzarella cheese. Bring ends of dough together over cheese, pinching to seal. Place seam side down on prepared baking sheet. Bake in center of oven 10 minutes or until golden brown. Makes 6 servings.

Skillet Spaghetti Pizza

1 pound bulk Italian sausage
1 tablespoon minced garlic
½ pound uncooked thin spaghetti, broken into 2-inch lengths
1 (26-ounce) jar spaghetti sauce
1½ cups water
1 cup (4 ounces) shredded mozzarella cheese
½ cup diced green bell pepper
1⅓ cups French's' French Fried Onions

Cook sausage and garlic in large nonstick skillet over medium heat until browned, stirring frequently; drain. Stir in uncooked spaghetti, spaghetti sauce and water. Bring to a boil; reduce heat to medium-low. Cover and simmer 15 minutes or until spaghetti is cooked, stirring occasionally. Top spaghetti mixture with cheese, bell pepper and French fried onions; remove from heat. Cover and let stand 3 minutes until cheese is melted. Serve immediately. Makes 8 servings.

My Own Pizza

Perfect sized pizzas just for you.

¼ pound ground beef
¾ cup tomato sauce
½ teaspoon oregano
¼ teaspoon salt
Pinch garlic salt
1 (12-ounce) can refrigerator biscuits
¾ cup grated cheese

Preheat oven to 450°. Place beef in skillet and stir with a fork to break up large pieces. Cook on medium heat until browned; drain. Add tomato sauce, oregano, salt and garlic salt. Pat out each biscuit on cookie sheet to form individual pizza crusts. Spread each biscuit with ground beef mixture. Sprinkle with grated cheese. Bake 10 minutes. Makes 10 servings.

what is your favorite
Halloween costume?

_____

Name_____ Age_____

Monster Mouths

1 teaspoon vegetable oil

1 medium onion, chopped

4 slices bacon, chopped

1 pound ground beef

2 medium plum tomatoes, seeded and chopped

½ teaspoon salt

¼ teaspoon black pepper

4 slices American cheese, chopped

½ (12-ounce) package jumbo pasta shells (about 18), cooked and drained

Baby carrots, olives, red bell pepper, small pickles and cheese slices for decoration

Preheat oven to 350°. Lightly grease a 9x13-inch baking dish. Heat oil in large skillet over medium heat. Add onion and bacon; cook until onion is tender. Add beef; cook and stir about 5 minutes or until beef is no longer pink. Stir in tomatoes, salt and pepper. Stir in cheese. Spoon mixture into cooked shells; place in prepared baking dish. Cut carrots into very thin strips. Cut small slit in olives; poke one end of thin carrot strip into olives for eyes. Cut red bell pepper into fang shapes. Slice pickle lengthwise into tongue shape. Cut cheese slice into zigzag pattern for teeth. Bake shells 3 to 5 minutes or until hot; remove from oven. Decorate as desired with olive and carrot eyes, bell pepper fangs, pickle tongue and cheese teeth. Serve immediately. Makes about 6 servings.

Toasted Pumpkin Seeds

Pumpkin seeds (about ¾ cup)
1½ tablespoons salt

Preheat oven to 300°. Remove seeds from pumpkin and wash in colander under warm water. Spread seeds on cookie sheet and sprinkle with salt (use more or less to taste). Bake 20 to 30 minutes or until seeds are dry and crisp, stirring occasionally. Let cool in pan. Store in airtight container.

Dinner in a Pumpkin

1 medium pumpkin
2 pounds ground beef, browned
¼ cup soy sauce
2 tablespoons packed brown sugar
1 (4-ounce) can mushrooms, optional
1 (10.75-ounce) can cream of chicken soup
2 cups hot cooked rice

Preheat oven to 375°. Clean out pumpkin reserving top for a lid. In a bowl, combine remaining ingredients except rice and put inside the pumpkin. Replace top of pumpkin and place in center of baking sheet. Bake 1 hour. Scoop out and serve over rice, scraping off a little of the pumpkin flesh too.

What does your Mom do?

_____

Name _____

Age _____

Easy & Amazing Roast

1 (3- to 4-pound) pot roast
1 (1-ounce) package original-style ranch dressing
1 (1-ounce) package zesty Italian dry dressing mix
1 (1-ounce) package brown gravy mix

Combine ranch, Italian and brown gravy packets with
½ cup water and pour over roast in a slow cooker. Cook
4 to 6 hours on medium. Easy, yes, but also amazing;
the roast will be super tender with a delicious gravy.
Don't forget the mashed potatoes.

Smothered Pork Chops

4 thick pork chops
½ cup uncooked rice
1 medium onion
Salt and pepper
1 lemon
1 (10.75-ounce) can cream of mushroom soup

Preheat oven to 325°. Trim fat from pork chops. Place chops in skillet over low heat and brown on both sides. Pour rice into large baking dish; place pork chops over rice. Cut onion into 4 slices; place 1 slice on each pork chop. Sprinkle with small amount of salt and pepper. Cut lemon into 4 slices; place on onion slices. Pour soup over pork chops. Cover and bake 1 hour.

Fritos Pie

2 pounds ground beef
½ onion, chopped
1 teaspoon black pepper
½ teaspoon garlic salt
2½ cups tomato sauce
1 (8-ounce) jar salsa
4 tablespoons chili
   seasoning mix
1 (15-ounce) can light red
   kidney beans, drained
1 (15-ounce) can dark red
   kidney beans, drained
1 (10.5-ounce) bag Fritos
   corn chips
1 (8-ounce) bag shredded
   Cheddar cheese

In a large saucepan over medium-high heat, sauté ground beef and onion 10 minutes or until meat browns. Drain off excess grease. Stir in pepper, garlic salt, tomato sauce, salsa, chili seasoning and kidney beans. Reduce heat and simmer 1 hour. Preheat oven to 350°. Lightly grease a 9x13-inch casserole dish. Layer Fritos on bottom of casserole. Spoon chili over Fritos and top with cheese. Bake 20 minutes. Makes 8 servings.

Trivets

Great gift idea and terrific Sunday school, vacation bible school, or a party project.

Paint markers
Bathroom tiles
Felt pads

Have children color on tiles with markers. Glue felt pad on bottom of each. Use as a trivet.

What is your favorite thing to do outside?

_____

Name_____ Age_____

Dinner Pie

Not just for dinner, this meaty and cheesy pie is great for breakfast, too.

1 pound bulk pork sausage or ground chuck
3 teaspoons minced garlic
2½ cups shredded Monterey Jack cheese, divided
1⅓ cups milk
3 eggs
¾ cup biscuit/baking mix
¾ teaspoon rubbed sage
¼ teaspoon pepper

In a large skillet, cook sausage over medium heat until meat is no longer pink. Add garlic; cook 1 minute longer. Drain. Stir in 2 cups cheese. Transfer to a greased 9-inch deep-dish pie plate. In a small bowl, combine milk, eggs, biscuit mix, sage and pepper. Pour over sausage mixture. Bake at 400° for 20 to 25 minutes or until a knife inserted near the center comes out clean. Sprinkle with remaining cheese; bake 1 to 2 minutes longer or until cheese is melted. Let stand 10 minutes before cutting.

Ham & Cheese Shells & Trees

2 tablespoons margarine or butter
1 (6.2 ounce) box Pasta Roni Shells & White Cheddar
2 cups fresh or frozen chopped broccoli
⅔ cup milk
1½ cups ham or cooked turkey, cut into thin strips (about
   6 ounces)

In large saucepan, bring 2 cups water and margarine to a boil. Stir in pasta. Reduce heat to medium. Gently boil, uncovered, 6 minutes, stirring occasionally. Stir in broccoli; return to a boil. Boil 6 to 8 minutes or until most of water is absorbed. Stir in milk, ham and special seasoning packet. Return to a boil; boil 1 to 2 minutes or until pasta is tender. Let stand 5 minutes before serving. Makes 4 servings.

Scalloped Potatoes and Ham

1 stick butter, melted
10 potatoes, peeled and diced
1 pound chopped ham
1 large onion, chopped

Milk
Garlic salt
Seasoning salt
2 teaspoons cornstarch

Place butter, potatoes, ham and onion in casserole dish. Cover with milk. Sprinkle with garlic salt and seasoning salt to taste. Sprinkle cornstarch over top and mix. Bake 1½ hours at 350° or until sauce is thickened.

What is your favorite app?

_____

_____

Name _____

Age _____

Would you like to ride in a Submarine?

☐ **Yes** ☐ **No** ☐ **Maybe**

What would you see?

_____

_____

_____

Name_____ Age_____

Chili Dog Pie

2½ cups baking mix
3 tablespoons prepared
   mustard
6 tablespoons water

1 (16-ounce) package hot dogs
2 (15-ounce) cans chili
½ cup shredded Cheddar
   cheese

Preheat oven to 425°. Grease a 9x13-inch pan. Combine baking mix, mustard and water; mix well. Press into pan and set aside. Cut hot dogs into bite-size pieces. Spread out on top of dough. Top with chili. Sprinkle with cheese. Bake 20 minutes.

Submarine Wieners

12 wieners
8 medium peeled potatoes

Mustard
12 slices pasteurized cheese

Boil wieners 3 minutes. Remove from water; drain well, then slit almost in half, leaving bottoms intact. Boil potatoes. Drain and mash until soft. Spread mustard on both cut sides of wieners. Press mashed potatoes into slit of wieners and top with slice of cheese. Bake at 350° until cheese melts. Serves 4.

Frankfurters in Batter

1 cup regular pancake mix
2 tablespoons cornmeal
1 tablespoon sugar
⅔ cup water
8 hot dogs
Cooking oil

Combine pancake mix, cornmeal, sugar and water; beat until smooth. Let batter stand 10 minutes. Pour 1 inch of cooking oil into an electric skillet and heat to 370° or heat oil over moderate heat in a regular frying pan. Dip hot dogs in batter, thoroughly coating all sides. Fry until brown and crisp. Drain on paper towels. Serves 4 to 8.

Crusted Frankfurters

8 hot dogs
8 slivers American or Cheddar cheese
1 (8-ounce) tube refrigerator crescent rolls

Halve hot dogs lengthwise, but not all the way through. Place cheese in split hot dogs. Separate crescent rolls. Place a hot dog on pointed tip of each roll, and roll up. Place on baking sheet and bake at 375° for 20 minutes. Serves 4 to 8.

Hot Diggity Dots & Twisters

⅔ cup milk

2 tablespoons margarine or butter

1 (4.8 ounce) package Pasta Roni Four Cheese Flavor with Corkscrew Pasta

1½ cups frozen peas

4 hot dogs, cut into ½-inch pieces

2 teaspoons mustard

In large saucepan, bring 1¼ cups water, milk and margarine just to a boil. Stir in pasta, special seasoning packet and peas; return to a boil. Reduce heat to medium. Gently boil, uncovered, 7 to 8 minutes or until pasta is tender, stirring occasionally. Stir in hot dogs and mustard. Let stand 3 to 5 minutes before serving. Makes 4 servings.

Bubbles

1 cup liquid dishwashing detergent (Dawn works great; don't use generic or store brands)

2 cups warm water

3 tablespoon glycerin (buy at drug store or with cake decorating supplies)

½ teaspoon sugar

Gently mix ingredients and store in a labeled, airtight container such as a clean glass spaghetti sauce jar or jelly jar. These homemade bubbles keep well. If the mixture sits for more than a few weeks, give the container a gentle swirl to combine the ingredients. Don't shake the container; you want to save those suds for your bubbles!

No fancy equipment needed. Just form your hand into a circle by connecting your pointer finger and thumb, dip into bubble mixture and blow. You can also use pre-manufactured bubble wands or make your own using pipe cleaners. If you use pipe cleaners, experiment with different shapes and sizes. Other options for wands are a slotted spoon, funnels, a silicone steaming basket, mason jar lid rings, cookie cutters, or wrap 3 straws together with tape—the options are endless.

These bubbles are durable and don't break easily, but are also sticky so are best used outside only. The mixture washes out of clothing.

Variations: Add a drop of food coloring for colored bubbles. These look great but shouldn't be used around anything that can be stained. Wear old clothes when blowing colored bubbles.

Glow-in-the-dark bubbles can be made by breaking open a yellow highlighter and letting the ink soak into the water. Bubbles will glow under a black light. If you use tonic water instead of regular water, the bubbles will glow pale blue under a black light.

Chicken Bombs

5 boneless, skinless chicken breasts
Salt to taste
Pepper to taste
1 (4-ounce) package cream cheese, softened
1 cup shredded Colby-Jack or Cheddar cheese
5 jalapeños, sliced in half lengthwise and cleaned
20 slices bacon
1 cup barbecue sauce

Slice chicken breasts in half (like a hamburger bun). Place pieces between wax paper and pound to ¼-inch thick. Season with salt and pepper. Combine cream cheese and shredded cheese. Spread cheese into pepper halves, using all cheese. Place stuffed 1 pepper half on each piece of chicken. Wrap chicken around pepper then wrap two pieces bacon around each (secure with a toothpick if needed). Cook on a preheated 350° grill over indirect heat 30 minutes or until chicken is done. Turn every 5 minutes basting with barbecue sauce each time. Or bake in the oven at 375° for 30 minutes or until chicken is done. Baste a couple times with barbecue sauce. Set oven to broil and broil 5 minutes before removing from oven to caramelize the sauce. Makes 10 servings.

What would you like to drive
for your first car?

_____

What color will it be?

_____

Who will be riding with you?

_____

Loaded Potato and Chicken Casserole

⅓ cup olive oil
1½ tablespoons salt
1 tablespoon black pepper
1 tablespoon paprika
2 tablespoons garlic powder
6 tablespoons hot sauce
8 to 10 medium potatoes, cut in ½-inch cubes
2 pounds boneless chicken breasts, cut in 1-inch cubes
1 cup cooked, crumbled bacon
1 cup diced green onion
2 cups fiesta blend cheese

Preheat oven to 500°. Spray a 9x13-inch baking dish with cooking spray. In a large bowl, combine olive oil, salt, pepper, paprika, garlic powder and hot sauce. Add cubed potatoes and stir to coat. Spoon potatoes into prepared baking dish, leaving behind as much of the hot sauce mixture as possible (reserve). Bake potatoes 45 to 50 minutes, stirring every 10 to 15 minutes, until cooked through (will be crispy and browned on outside). While potatoes are cooking, add cubed chicken to bowl with leftover sauce and stir to coat. Once potatoes are fully cooked, remove from oven and lower temperature to 400°. Top cooked potatoes with raw marinated chicken. In a bowl, combine bacon and green onion; spread over raw chicken. Return casserole to oven and bake 15 minutes or until chicken is cooked through. Top with cheese and return to oven just until cheese is melted.

Name_____

Age _____

television

What is on the news today?

_____

_____

_____

_____

Name_____ Age_____

Oven-Baked Chicken Parmesan

4 boneless, skinless chicken breast halves
1 egg, lightly beaten
¾ cup Italian-seasoned dry breadcrumbs
1 (26-ounce) jar Ragú Old World Style Pasta Sauce
1 cup shredded mozzarella cheese

Preheat oven to 400°. Dip chicken in egg and then in breadcrumbs, coating well. Arrange chicken in a 9x13-inch glass baking dish. Bake uncovered 20 minutes. Pour pasta sauce over chicken and top with cheese. Bake an additional 10 minutes or until chicken is thoroughly cooked. Makes 4 servings.

Parmesan-Crusted Chicken

½ cup mayonnaise
½ cup grated Parmesan cheese
4 boneless, skinless chicken breast halves
1 cup Italian-seasoned dry breadcrumbs

Preheat oven to 425°. Combine mayonnaise with Parmesan in medium bowl. Arrange chicken on baking sheet. Evenly top with mayonnaise mixture and sprinkle with breadcrumbs. Bake 20 minutes or until chicken is thoroughly cooked.

Hand Print

½ cup salt

¾ cup hot water

2 cups flour

1 tablespoon oil

Pie tin

Pencil

Paint, crayons, white glue,
    glitter or markers

Ribbon

Dissolve salt in hot water. Add flour and oil; mix together. Knead well. Put dough in pie tin. Flatten dough so it reaches edges. Touch-test to ensure it is not too hot for your child to touch. Press child's hand in dough to make a deep hand print. Make a small hole near the top. Use your finger or tip of a pencil to write child's name in the dough. Bake at 300° for about 1 hour. Cool then decorate with paint, crayons, glitter or markers. Tie a ribbon through the hole and hang up to enjoy for years to come.

Golden Chicken Nuggets

1 pound boneless, skinless chicken, cut into 1½-inch pieces
¼ cup French's Sweet & Tangy Honey Mustard
2 cups French's French Fried Onions, finely crushed

Preheat oven to 400°. Toss chicken with mustard in medium bowl. Place French fried onions into resealable plastic food storage bag. Toss chicken in onions, a few pieces at a time, pressing gently to adhere. Place nuggets in shallow baking pan. Bake 15 minutes or until chicken is no longer pink in center. Serve with additional honey mustard. Makes 4 servings.

Chicken Dinner Winner

This chicken dinner is a winner on taste and because it's super-easy. If you don't like the heat, replace the Rotel with a can of chopped tomatoes.

1 (16-ounce) can chicken broth	Garlic powder
1 (10-ounce) can Rotel tomatoes	Salt and pepper
1 cup uncooked white rice	1 cup shredded Cheddar cheese
1 pound chicken tenders	

Pour chicken broth and Rotel in a large, deep skillet with a cover. Stir in rice. Lay chicken tenders on top of rice and sprinkle with garlic powder, salt and pepper. Cover and cook over medium-high heat 20 minutes or until chicken is opaque. Remove from heat and sprinkle with cheese. Stir lightly until cheese melts slightly. Makes 4 to 6 servings.

What is your favorite food?

At Home _____

Takeout _____

Name_____ Age_____

Chicken Tenders with Creamy Honey Mustard

⅓ cup all-purpose flour
1 large egg, lightly beaten
Coarse salt and ground pepper
4 cups crisp rice cereal
2 tablespoons olive oil
1½ pounds chicken tenders

½ cup sour cream
2 tablespoons Dijon mustard
1 tablespoon honey
4 medium carrots, cut into sticks
1 cucumber, halved lengthwise,
   seeded and cut into sticks

Preheat oven to 475°. Place flour in a shallow bowl and egg in another bowl; season both with salt and pepper. Pulse cereal and oil in a food processor until fine crumbs form. Season with salt and pepper; transfer to a third shallow bowl. Coat chicken first in flour, shaking off excess; then in egg, letting excess drip off; and finally in cereal mixture, pressing to help it adhere. Place on a baking sheet and bake until light golden brown and cooked through, 10 to 15 minutes, turning over halfway through. Meanwhile, in a small bowl, mix together sour cream, mustard and honey; season with salt and pepper. Serve tenders and vegetables with creamy honey mustard on the side.

Crispy Cheddar Chicken

2 pounds chicken tenders or 4 large
   chicken breasts
2 sleeves Ritz crackers
½ cup milk
3 cups grated Cheddar cheese
¼ teaspoon salt

⅛ teaspoon pepper
1 teaspoon dried parsley
1 (10-ounce) can cream of chicken
   soup
2 tablespoons sour cream
2 tablespoons butter

If using chicken breasts instead of tenders, cut each chicken breast into 3 pieces. Treat a 9x13-inch pan with nonstick cooking spray. Crush crackers into a shallow bowl. Place milk and cheese into 2 separate shallow bowls. Add salt and pepper to cracker crumbs and stir to mix. Dip each piece of chicken into milk and then cheese pressing cheese into chicken with your fingers. Coat with crackers, again pressing the crumbs to adhere to chicken. Lay chicken inside treated pan. Sprinkle with dried parsley. Cover pan with foil and bake at 400° for 35 minutes. Remove foil and bake an additional 10 to 15 minutes or until chicken ks golden brown and crispy. In a medium-size saucepan, combine soup, sour cream and butter with a whisk. Cook over medium-high heat, stirring frequently, until hot and smooth. Serve chicken topped with sauce. Makes 6 to 8 servings.

Where is your favorite place to go on vacation?

_____

_____

Chicken Hawaiian

2 (3-pound) broilers, cut up
Salt and pepper
1 (15-ounce) can pineapple chunks, including juice
½ cup soy sauce
4 tablespoons cooking oil
1 (12-ounce) jar preserved kumquats, including juice

Place chicken pieces in a large plastic container with a lid; season with salt and pepper to taste. Cover with pineapple chunks (with juice) and soy sauce; refrigerate overnight. Drain chicken, reserving marinade. In a large skillet, working in batches, sauté chicken in cooking oil until browned. Transfer to a 3-quart casserole. Cover with marinade and kumquats (with juice). Bake, uncovered, at 350° for 1 hour. Serves 6.

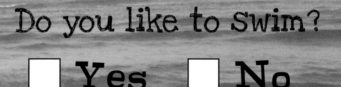

Do you like to swim?

☐ **Yes**   ☐ **No**

Name_____ Age_____

Chicken-on-a-Stick

1 egg
1 cup milk
1½ cups flour
Salt to taste
Lemon pepper to taste
Garlic powder to taste

4 boneless, skinless
 chicken breasts
1 large onion
1 medium potato
Oil
Wooden skewers

Beat egg and milk together; set aside. Season flour with salt, lemon pepper and garlic powder and set aside. Cut chicken into chunks. Quarter onions and pull apart. Slice potatoes thin (do not peel). Heat enough oil for deep-frying. Thread chicken, onion and potatoes onto wooden skewers till full. Dip in egg wash, then roll in seasoned flour. Fry in oil till done. Drain on paper towels.

Have you ever been in a parade?

☐ Yes   ☐ No

Delicious Drumsticks

½ cup all-purpose flour
1 teaspoon salt
½ teaspoon paprika
¼ teaspoon pepper
6 chicken drumsticks (about 1½ pounds)
¼ cup margarine or butter, melted and cooled

Heat oven to 425°. Mix flour, salt, paprika and pepper in a bowl. Dip chicken drumsticks into margarine, roll in flour mixture to coat. Arrange in an ungreased 8x8-inch pan. Bake, uncovered, until done, about 50 minutes. Serves 2 to 4.

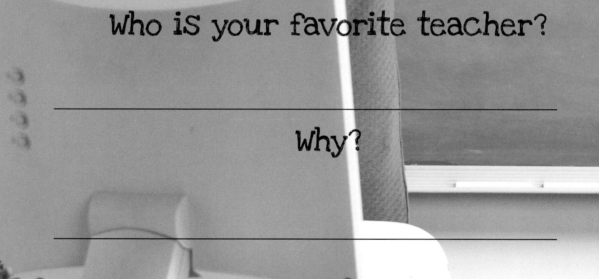

Who is your favorite teacher?

_____

Why?

_____

Name _____

Grade _____

Chicken and Dumpling Casserole

This easy recipe can be made even easier by using store-bought rotisserie chicken which also gives the casserole a unique flavor.

½ stick butter
2 chicken breasts, cooked and shredded
1 teaspoon black pepper
½ teaspoon dried sage
2 cups milk
2 cups Bisquick
2 cups chicken broth
3 teaspoons Wyler's chicken granules
1 (10.75-ounce) can cream of chicken soup

Preheat oven to 350°. In 9x13-inch casserole dish, melt butter. Spread shredded chicken over butter. Sprinkle with pepper and sage. Do not stir. In small bowl, mix milk and Bisquick. Slowly pour over chicken. Do not stir. In medium bowl, whisk together chicken broth, chicken granules and soup. Once blended, slowly pour over the Bisquick layer. Do not stir. Bake casserole 30 to 40 minutes or until dumplings on top are golden brown.

Where did you go on your first overnight trip?

_____

How old were you?

_____

Did you have fun?
☐ **Yes** ☐ **No**

Name _____

Rotel Chicken Mexican Casserole

1 (10-ounce) can Rotel tomatoes
1 (10.75-ounce) can cream of chicken soup
1 (4-ounce) can chopped green chiles
1 pound Velveeta or American cheese, cubed
3 split fryer breasts, cooked and cubed
1 (12-ounce) bag tortilla chips, crushed

Combine Rotel, soup, green chiles and cheese. Heat in microwave till melted; add chicken. In a casserole dish, layer half the tortilla chips and half the chicken mixture. Repeat layers (reserving a few chips for top) and top with a few crushed chips. Bake at 350° until hot and bubbly.

Mexican Chicken

1 pound boneless chicken breasts
1 teaspoon taco seasoning
Salt to taste
½ cup enchilada sauce
4 ounces Cheddar
  cheese, shredded
3 green onions,
  chopped

Sprinkle chicken on both sides with taco seasoning; grill or sauté until cooked through. Cut chicken into cubes and place in a greased 8x8-inch baking dish; season with salt to taste. Add enchilada sauce and toss to coat chicken. Sprinkle cheese over chicken and bake at 350° for 10 to 20 minutes or until hot and bubbly. Scatter green onions over top. Makes 4 servings.

Chicken & Cheese Enchiladas with Green Chili & Sour Cream Sauce

2 cups cooked, shredded chicken
2 cups shredded Monterey Jack cheese, divided
10 soft taco shells or small flour tortillas
3 tablespoons butter
3 tablespoons flour
2 cups chicken broth
1 cup sour cream
1 (4-ounce) can diced green chiles

Preheat oven to 350°. Grease a 9x13-inch pan. Mix chicken and 1 cup cheese. Roll up in taco shells and place in pan. In a saucepan, melt butter, stir in flour and cook 1 minute. Add broth and whisk until smooth. Heat over medium heat until thick and bubbly. Stir in sour cream and chiles. Do not bring to a boil or the sour cream will curdled. Pour over enchiladas and top with remaining cheese. Cover and bake 25 minutes. Remove foil and broil 3 minutes to brown the cheese.

What is your favorite hiding place?

_____

Name_____ Age_____

Hummingbird Food

1 part sugar
4 parts water
Red food coloring

Boil sugar and water until sugar is dissolved. When cool, mix in a few drops food coloring at a time until the liquid is as red as you want. Pour into hummingbird feeder.

Hummingbird Cake

CAKE:

3 cups all-purpose flour
1½ cups sugar
1 teaspoon baking soda
1 teaspoon salt
1½ teaspoons ground cinnamon
3 eggs
2 teaspoons vanilla extract

1½ cups canola oil
1 (8-ounce) can crushed pineapple, undrained
2 cups mashed bananas, about 3 large
1½ cups chopped pecans

Combine flour, sugar, baking soda, salt and cinnamon. Mix together with a whisk. Add eggs, vanilla extract, oil, pineapple, bananas and pecans. Mix with a spoon until all ingredients are wet. Spray 3 (9-inch) round cake pans or a 9x13-inch pan. Pour batter into pans and bake in preheated 350° oven 30 to 35 minutes until cake is done in center.

CREAM CHEESE FROSTING (double if you will be frosting 3 layers):

1 (8-ounce) package cream cheese, softened
2 cups powdered sugar

1 stick butter or margarine, softened
1 teaspoon vanilla

Whip all frosting ingredients together with mixer until smooth and of spreading consistency. Frost cake after it has cooled.

Balloon Celebration Cake

3 cups all-purpose flour
2 cups sugar
½ cup cocoa
2 teaspoons baking soda
1 teaspoon salt
⅔ cup vegetable oil
2 teaspoons vinegar
1 teaspoon vanilla
2 cups cold water
1 (16-ounce) tub ready-to-spread
   frosting (any flavor)
Pastel mint wafers, flattened
   gumdrops or fruit gems
Shoestring licorice

Heat oven to 350°. Grease 2 (9-inch) round cake pans and dust with flour. Mix flour, sugar, cocoa, baking soda and salt in a large bowl. Mix oil, vinegar and vanilla. Stir oil mixture and water into flour mixture real hard until well blended, about 1 minute. Immediately pour batter into pans, dividing evenly. Bake until wooden pick inserted in center comes out clean, about 35 minutes. Let cool in pans 10 minutes. Remove cake from pans; cool completely. Fill and frost as directed on frosting tub. Arrange wafer "balloons" on top of cake using licorice for balloon strings.

Strawberry Lemonade Cake

1 box strawberry cake mix, plus ingredients to prepare
1 (8-ounce) package cream cheese, softened
1 (0.23-ounce) packet Kool-Aid Lemonade
Yellow food coloring gel
1 (16-ounce) jar marshmallow creme
1 (8-ounce) container Cool Whip
Fresh strawberries for garnish

Make cake according to directions on box and bake in 2 (9-inch) round cake pans. Turn finished cakes out on cooling racks and allow to cool completely. Cream together cream cheese and lemonade mix until smooth. Add food coloring to desired shade. Mix in marshmallow creme and then mix in Cool Whip until completely smooth. Refrigerate until cake has cooled. Cut each cake layer in half horizontally. Alternating layers of cake with layers of filling, assemble cake. End with layer of filling. Top with sliced strawberries. Refrigerate and serve chilled.

Popcorn Cake

4 quarts (16 cups) popped popcorn
1 pound spiced gumdrops
½ cup dry roasted peanuts
½ cup butter or margarine
½ cup vegetable oil
1 (1-pound) package marshmallows

Combine popcorn, gumdrops and peanuts in large bowl. In a saucepan, melt butter. Mix in oil and marshmallows. Heat, stirring, until marshmallows are melted. Pour over popcorn. Mix well. Press into greased springform pan. Serve immediately.

What is your favorite dessert?

_____

Name_____ Age_____

Banana Fudge Layer Cake

1 package Duncan Hines Moist Deluxe Yellow Cake Mix

1⅓ cups water

3 eggs

⅓ cup vegetable oil

1 cup mashed ripe bananas, about 3 medium

1 (16-ounce) container Duncan Hines Chocolate Frosting

Preheat oven to 350°. Grease and flour 2 (9-inch) round cake pans. Combine cake mix, water, eggs and oil in large bowl. Beat at low speed with electric mixer until moistened. Beat at medium speed 2 minutes. Stir in bananas. Pour into prepared pans. Bake at 350° for 28 to 31 minutes or until toothpick inserted in center comes out clean. Cool in pans 15 minutes. Remove from pans; cool completely. Fill and frost cake with frosting. Garnish as desired. Makes 12 to 16 servings.

Cream Puff Cake

1 stick margarine

1 cup water

1 cup flour

4 eggs

1 (5.1-ounce) box instant vanilla or
  white chocolate pudding

3 cups milk

1 (8-ounce) package cream cheese,
  softened

1 (8-ounce) carton Cool Whip

Chocolate syrup

Boil margarine and water together. Add flour and mix well. Cool slightly and stir in eggs, 1 at a time. Mix well and spread into a greased 9x13-inch pan. Bake at 400° for 30 minutes. Cool completely. In a large bowl, mix pudding, milk and cream cheese. Beat until lumps disappear. Pour into cream puff crust. Spread Cool Whip on top of pudding and drizzle with syrup. Refrigerate. This keeps well for days.

Singing Cake

This cake only sings while it bakes and only if the ingredients and directions are followed exactly.

1 cup butter
2 cups brown sugar
3 eggs, separated
2 (1-ounce) squares
    unsweetened chocolate,
    melted
1 cup raisins

2 teaspoons cinnamon
1 teaspoon cloves
4 cups sifted flour
1 cup chopped nuts
1 cup strawberry jam
2 teaspoons baking powder
1 cup buttermilk

Grease and flour an angel food cake pan. Preheat oven to 350°. Cream butter and sugar. Add egg yolks and stir. Add melted chocolate and stir. Add raisins and stir. Add cinnamon, cloves and flour; stir. Add nuts and jam; stir. Beat egg whites until stiff and set aside. Mix baking powder into the buttermilk; quickly add to the cake mixture and stir. Fold in beaten egg whites. Quickly pour batter into prepared pan. Bake until cake stops singing, about 45 minutes.

What is your favorite song?

Who sings your favorite song?

_____

Do you like to sing?

☐ **Yes** ☐ **No**

☐ Only when nobody
is listening

Dr. Pepper Cake

1 box yellow cake mix
1 (3.9-ounce) box instant vanilla pudding
4 eggs
¾ cup oil
1 (10-ounce) can Dr. Pepper plus more for Glaze
¾ cup chopped walnuts

GLAZE:
1 cup powdered sugar
1 teaspoon vanilla

Heat oven to 350°. Grease a Bundt pan. Mix cake ingredients together and pour into Bundt pan. Bake 1 hour. Mix powdered sugar, vanilla and enough Dr. Pepper to make a thin glaze. After cake cools, pour glaze over the top. Cut and serve.

What is your favorite soda?

☐ Sprite   ☐ Coke

☐ Orange   ☐ Grape

☐ Something else

Double Chocolate Coca-Cola Cake

1 cup Coca-Cola (regular, not diet)
½ cup oil
1 stick butter
3 tablespoons cocoa
2 cups sugar

2 cups flour
½ teaspoon salt
2 eggs
½ cup buttermilk
1 teaspoon baking soda
1 teaspoon vanilla

FROSTING:

1 stick butter
3 tablespoons cocoa
6 tablespoons cream or milk

1 teaspoon vanilla extract
3¾ cups powdered sugar

In a saucepan, mix Coca-Cola, oil, butter and cocoa and bring to a boil. In another bowl, combine sugar, flour and salt. Pour boiling cola mixture over flour mixture and beat well. Add eggs, buttermilk, baking soda and vanilla and beat well. Pour mixture into a greased and floured 9x13-inch baking pan and bake at 350° for 20 to 25 minutes. Remove from oven. Cool about 10 minutes before frosting.

For frosting, combine butter, cocoa and milk in a saucepan over medium heat. Cook until butter melts. Beat in remaining ingredients and spread over cake while warm.

Chocolate Banana Cake

CAKE:
1 box Duncan Hines Moist Deluxe Devils Food Cake Mix
3 eggs
1½ cups milk
½ cup vegetable oil

Preheat oven to 350°. Grease and flour a 9x13-inch pan. Combine cake mix, eggs, milk and oil in large bowl. Beat at low speed with electric mixer until moistened. Beat at medium speed 2 minutes. Pour into pan. Bake 35 to 38 minutes or until toothpick inserted in center comes out clean. Cool completely.

TOPPING:
1 (3.4-ounce) package banana cream instant pudding and pie filling
1 cup milk
1 cup whipping cream, whipped
1 medium banana
Lemon juice
Chocolate sprinkles for garnish

Combine pudding mix and milk in large bowl. Stir until smooth. Fold in whipped cream. Spread on top of cooled cake. Slice banana; dip in lemon juice and arrange on top. Garnish with chocolate sprinkles. Refrigerate until ready to serve. Makes 12 to 16 servings.

What is the best Christmas gift you ever received?

_____

Who gave it to you?

_____

Name_____ Age_____

Magic Balloon Treats

Wrapped chocolate
candy, jelly beans
or other wrapped
candy

Balloons

Craft glue

Colored yarn

Insert a few pieces candy into balloon and inflate slightly (only about 3 inches long). Mix equal parts craft glue with water. Dip yarn into glue mixture and wrap around balloon until evenly covered. When yarn is dry, pop or let air out of balloon. Discard balloon and you will have a pretty ball with candy on the inside.

Kids' Confetti Cake

CAKE:

1 box Duncan Hines Moist Deluxe Classic Yellow Cake Mix

1 (3.4-ounce) package instant vanilla pudding and pie filling

4 eggs

1 cup water

½ cup vegetable oil

1 cup mini semisweet chocolate chips

Preheat oven to 350°. Grease and flour a 9x13-inch baking pan. Combine cake mix, pudding mix, eggs, water and oil in large bowl. Beat at medium speed with electric mixer 2 minutes. Stir in chocolate chips. Pour into prepared pan. Bake 40 to 45 minutes or until toothpick inserted in center comes out clean. Top immediately while cake is still hot.

TOPPING:

1 cup colored miniature marshmallows

⅔ cup Duncan Hines Creamy Home-Style Chocolate Frosting

2 tablespoons mini semisweet chocolate chips

Immediately arrange marshmallows evenly over hot cake. Place frosting in microwave-safe bowl. Microwave on high (100% power) 25 to 30 seconds. Stir until smooth. Drizzle evenly over marshmallows and cake. Sprinkle with chocolate chips. Cool completely. Makes 12 to 16 servings.

What is your favorite saying?

_____

_____

Name_____ Age_____

Dirt Cake

2 (15-ounce) packages Oreo cookies
4 tablespoons butter or margarine, softened
1 (8-ounce) package cream cheese, softened
1 cup powdered sugar
3½ cups milk
2 (3-ounce) packages instant French vanilla pudding
1 (12-ounce) container Cool Whip, container reserved
1 (8-inch) flowerpot

Finely crush cookies and set aside. Cream together butter, cream cheese and powdered sugar. In a separate bowl, mix milk, pudding and non-dairy whipped topping. Using a hand mixer, combine butter and pudding mixtures. Put empty Cool Whip container into flowerpot. Fill with alternate layers of cookies and pudding mixture, ending with cookies on top. Refrigerate. When ready to serve, place a new artificial flower (clean stem well) into pudding.

Captivating Caterpillar Cupcakes

1 box Duncan Hines Moist Deluxe White Cake Mix

3 egg whites

1½ cups water

2 tablespoons vegetable oil

½ cup star decors, divided

1 (16-ounce) container Duncan Hines Vanilla Frosting

Green food coloring

6 chocolate sandwich cookies, finely crushed*

½ cup candy-coated chocolate pieces

⅓ cup assorted jelly beans

Assorted nonpareil decors (cookie/cake decorations)

Preheat oven to 350°. Place paper liners in 24 muffin cups. Combine cake mix, egg whites, water and oil in large bowl. Beat at low speed with electric mixer until moistened. Beat at medium speed 2 minutes. Fold in ⅓ cup star decors. Fill paper liners about half full. Bake 18 to 23 minutes until toothpick inserted in center comes out clean. Cool in pan 5 minutes. Remove and cool completely on racks.

Tint frosting with green food coloring. Frost 1 cupcake. Sprinkle ½ teaspoon chocolate cookie crumbs on frosting. Arrange 4 candy-coated chocolate pieces to form caterpillar body. Place a jelly bean at 1 end to form head. Attach remaining star and nonpareil decors with dots of frosting to form eyes. Repeat with remaining cupcakes. Makes 24 cupcakes.

Tip: To finely crush chocolate sandwich cookies, place cookies in resealable plastic bag. Remove excess air from bag; seal. Press rolling pin on top of cookies to break into pieces. Continue pressing until evenly crushed.

What do you like to do after school?

_____

_____

Name_____ Age_____

Cookies & Cream Cupcakes

2¼ cups all-purpose flour

1 tablespoon baking powder

½ teaspoon salt

1⅔ cups sugar

1 cup milk

½ cup (1 stick) butter, softened

2 teaspoons vanilla

3 egg whites

1 cup crushed chocolate sandwich cookies (about 10) plus additional for garnish

1 (16-ounce) container vanilla frosting

Preheat oven to 350°. Lightly grease 24 standard (2½-inch) muffin pan cups or line with paper liners. Sift flour, baking powder and salt together in large bowl. Stir in sugar. Add milk, butter and vanilla. Beat with electric mixer at low speed 30 seconds. Beat at medium speed 2 minutes. Add egg whites; beat 2 minutes. Stir in 1 cup crushed cookies. Spoon batter evenly into prepared muffin cups. Bake 20 to 25 minutes or until toothpicks inserted into centers come out clean. Cool in pans on wire racks 10 minutes. Remove to racks; cool completely. Frost cupcakes; garnish with additional crushed cookies.

Ice Cream Cone Cakes

1 box cake mix (preferred flavor), plus ingredients to prepare
24 flat-bottom ice cream cones

Prepare cake mix as directed on package. Spoon about ¼ cup batter into each cone. Set cones on baking sheet. Bake at 350° for 25 minutes. Cool on rack.

FLUFFY PUDDING FROSTING:

1 cup cold milk
1 (3.4-ounce) package instant pudding mix (preferred flavor)
¼ cup powdered sugar
1 (8-ounce) container non-dairy whipped topping
Sprinkles, optional

Beat milk, pudding mix and powdered sugar together. Fold in non-dairy whipped topping. Spoon frosting over cakes. Decorate with sprinkles if desired. Serve immediately. (Do not frost until ready to serve. Frosting may be stored in the refrigerator up to 3 days. Stir well before frosting Ice Cream Cone Cakes.)

where do
you like to shop?

_____

Who do you like to shop with?

_____

Name_____ Age_____

Birthday Hats

1 box cake mix (any flavor), plus ingredients to prepare
2 (16-ounce) containers vanilla frosting, divided
Food coloring
24 sugar ice cream cones
Colored Sugar, sprinkles or other cake decorations

Line 24 standard muffin pan cups with paper liners or spray with nonstick cooking spray. Prepare cake mix and bake in muffin cups according to package directions. Cool in pans on wire racks 15 minutes. Remove cupcakes from pans; cool completely on wire racks. Frost cupcakes using 1 container of vanilla frosting.

Tint remaining frosting your preferred color (or half and tint each half a different color). Cover cones in frosting. Place 1 cone upside down on each frosted cupcake, and decorate with colored sugar, sprinkles, and other cake decorations.

Tell me about your last birthday party.

_____

_____

_____

Name_____ Age_____

Oreo Brownie Cupcakes

Super easy and looks and tastes delicious.

1 box brownie mix, plus ingredients to prepare
48 Oreos
Peanut butter

Preheat oven to 350°. Prepare brownie mix according to package directions (do not cook); set aside. Line 2 (12-cup) muffin tins with cupcake liners. Spread peanut butter on top of one Oreo and place in bottom up one cupcake liner. Spread peanut butter over a second Oreo and place on top of first (peanut butter side up). Repeat until muffin tins are full. Pour brownie mix over cookie stacks to fill muffin three quarters full. Bake 20 minutes. Remove from oven and cool before serving.

Cobweb Cups

1 package brownie mix, plus
  ingredients to prepare
½ cup mini chocolate chips
2 ounces cream cheese,
  softened
1 egg, beaten
2 tablespoons sugar
2 tablespoons all-purpose
  flour
¼ teaspoon vanilla

Preheat oven to 350°. Line 18 standard muffin pans with paper liners. Prepare brownie mix according to package directions for cake-like brownies. Stir in chocolate chips. Spoon batter evenly into prepared muffin pans. Combine cream cheese and egg in small bowl. Add sugar, flour and vanilla; beat until well mixed. Place cream cheese mixture in quart-size, zip-close plastic bag; seal bag. Snip off small corner from 1 side of bag. Pipe cream cheese mixture in concentric circle design on each cupcake plus a dot in the center. Draw toothpick through cream cheese mixture, from the center out, 6 to 8 times, making a web design. Bake 20 to 25 minutes or until toothpick inserted into center comes out clean. Cool in pans on wire racks 15 minutes. Remove to racks; cool completely.

Fun Homemade Clay

1 cup salt
½ cup cornstarch
1 cup water

Wax paper
Watercolors, tempera paints,
    food coloring

Mix salt, cornstarch and water in a saucepan. Boil to soft ball stage (234° to 240° on a candy thermometer). Remove to wax paper and allow to cool enough to handle. Knead on wax paper until dough-like. Use immediately or wrap in wet cloth to keep for a few days. Mold clay into desired shapes and paint with watercolors or tempera paints. Or make different colors by adding food coloring to portions when kneading it. Great for free play or making Christmas decorations, animals and so much more.

Frog Cupcakes

1 package white cake mix, plus ingredients to prepare
1 (16-ounce) can vanilla frosting
6 drops green food coloring, or as needed
¼ cup green decorator sugar
12 large marshmallows
1 drop red food coloring
48 semisweet chocolate chips

Bake cupcakes according to package directions. Allow to cool completely. Scoop two thirds of the frosting into a small bowl and mix with green food coloring. Frost the cupcakes. Sprinkle some of the green sugar over the tops. Cut the marshmallows in half to make 2 circles. Dip half of each marshmallow piece into water and dip into the green sugar to make the eyelids. The remaining white part will be the eyes. Place on the cupcakes. Use a dot of white icing to glue a chocolate chip into the center of each eye for the pupil. Mix the remaining frosting with red food coloring to make pink. Use the pink icing to draw smiling mouths and nostrils or even tongues on the frogs.

"I Can't Believe You Used Up My Whole Box of Cereal" Squares

3 tablespoons margarine
6 cups (10.5 ounces) miniature marshmallows
½ cup peanut butter
5 cups Cheerios or Fruit Loops

Grease a 9x13-inch pan. In a large microwave-safe bowl, melt margarine. Add marshmallows and peanut butter; mix well. Microwave 2 minutes and stir. (If marshmallows are not fully melted, continue to heat in 30 second intervals, stirring well after each, until completely melted.) Immediately add cereal and stir carefully to completely coat without breaking up cereal. Using a greased spatula or wax paper, press mixture into greased pan. Cool and cut into squares.

Draw your favorite cereal—
right on the box!

Space Balls

1 cup smooth peanut butter
1 cup dried milk
1 cup crushed graham crackers
½ cup honey
Chopped nuts, flake coconut, melted chocolate, optional

Mix peanut butter, milk, graham crackers and honey together well. Shape into bite-size balls. Roll in nuts or coconut. Chill. Can be dipped in melted chocolate after being chilled.

Shooting stars are rocks called meteoroids.
Color these meteorites.

Shooting Stars

½ cup vanilla, milk chocolate
   or peanut butter morsels

¼ cup chopped toasted almonds

1 cup canned thin chow mein noodles

Candy-coated chocolate covered candies or mini semisweet
   chocolate morsels

Melt morsels in microwave for 50 to 70 seconds, stirring twice. Stir in almonds. Remove mixture to bowl. Stir in chow mein noodles. Use a teaspoon to scoop out a little of the mixture and place on wax paper or lightly greased baking sheet. Press several candies into each shooting star. Let stand at room temperature until set.

Would you like to be an astronaut?
☐ **Yes** ☐ **No**

Have you ever been bird watching?

☐ **Yes** ☐ **No**

What did you see?

_____

What is your favorite bird?

_____

Name_____

_____

Age _____

Birds' Nests

2 (8-ounce) milk chocolate bars
1 (6-ounce) package chow mein noodles
Frosting, optional
1 (9-ounce) package jelly beans

In saucepan over medium heat or in microwave, melt chocolate bars. Stir in noodles and shape into nests on wax paper. Place frosting, if desired, in nests and put in jelly beans for eggs; chill.

Help every bird get back to the birdhouse village.

Bird Cake

This cake is "for the birds" and should not be consumed by humans. It's a fun project that is super-fun when you watch the birds enjoy it.

1 cup plain flour
1 cup cornmeal
1 cup dry oats
½ cup milk
¼ cup raisins
¼ cup unsalted peanuts
½ cup peanut butter

Combine flour, cornmeal and oats in a bowl; stir in milk until well mixed. Add raisins and peanuts. Blend in peanut butter. Fill muffin cups half full and bake at 350° for 45 to 60 minutes, or until brown. Cool completely. Put out for the birds and find a quiet place to bird watch.

Pretzel Pecan Turtles

6 small pretzels
6 Rolo chewy caramels in milk chocolate, unwrapped
6 pecan halves

Line a microwave-safe plate with waxed paper. Place pretzels on plate, not touching. Top each with a Rolo. Microwave at 50% power for 30 seconds. Using a spoon, test to see if the candy is soft enough to easily press down; if not, microwave an additional 10 seconds at 50% power. Place a pecan over top and gently press down. (If your family doesn't like pecans, use a second pretzel on top instead.) This can also be made in the oven by baking at 350° for 3 to 5 minutes before placing the pecan on top.

Pecan Candy

2 cups pecans
2 tablespoons margarine, melted
2 (3-ounce) packages cream cheese
1 (16-ounce) box powdered sugar
1 teaspoon vanilla extract

Stir pecans into melted margarine then distribute into a single layer on a baking sheet. Toast 15 minutes in a 350° oven. Melt cream cheese in a double boiler. Add powdered sugar, vanilla extract and toasted pecans. Stir until well blended. Pour in buttered 8-inch dish. Cool completely. Cut into squares before serving.

Creamy New Orleans Pralines

A favorite Cajun candy that you will love, too.

3 cups sugar
1 cup buttermilk
¼ cup light corn syrup
1 pinch salt

1 teaspoon baking soda
1 teaspoon vanilla extract
4 cups pecans

Combine sugar, buttermilk, corn syrup and salt in a very large pan (it will foam considerably when soda is added) and bring to a nice rolling boil. Add soda, stir and cook until a drop forms a soft ball when dropped in cold water (234° to 240° on a candy thermometer), then remove from heat and add vanilla. Beat until color changes and candy thickens. Stir in pecans. Drop by teaspoons on greased cookie sheet (do it fast before the candy hardens).

What trick would you perform if you were a magician?

_____

Would like to make Someone disappear?

☐ Yes   ☐ No

If you pulled a bunny out of hat, what would you name it?

_____

Magic Delight

40 saltine crackers
1 cup packed brown sugar
1 cup butter (no substitutes)

1 (6-ounce) package chocolate chips
½ cup chopped nuts, optional

Place layer of crackers on a 10x15-inch foil-lined jelly-roll pan. Boil sugar and butter 3 minutes. Pour over crackers. Bake at 350° for 5 minutes or until crackers float. Sprinkle chocolate chips over crackers. When melted, spread and top with nuts. Cool and cut into bars.

Easiest Fudge Recipe in the World

You can't mess this up if you tried.

1 (14-ounce) can Eagle Brand condensed milk
3 cups semi-sweet chocolate chips
1½ teaspoons vanilla extract
1 cup chopped walnuts, optional

Combine condensed milk and chocolate chips in a microwave-safe bowl. Heat in 90 second intervals, stirring well each time, until melted and creamy. Stir in vanilla and walnuts. Pour into a treated 8x8-inch baking dish. Refrigerate 2 hours; cut and serve.

Variations: This simple recipe can be made many different ways. Substitute your favorite nut for the walnuts—pecans or peanuts or almonds or cashews (or a mixture). Use milk chocolate or dark chocolate chips for different flavors. You can even make it with peanut butter or white chocolate chips. For Dreamsicle Fudge, substitute the vanilla for orange flavoring when using white chocolate chips.

Homemade Reese's Cups

3 cups crunchy peanut butter
1½ (16-ounce) boxes powdered sugar
2 sticks margarine, softened
16 ounces dipping chocolate

Mix peanut butter, sugar and margarine thoroughly. Shape into marble-size balls. Melt dipping chocolate in top of double boiler. Dip each ball and place on wax paper.

Fudge Meltaways

¾ cup butter plus 1 teaspoon, divided
3½ (1-ounce) squares unsweetened chocolate, divided
¼ cup sugar
1 egg, beaten
2 teaspoons vanilla extract, divided
2 cups graham cracker crumbs
1 cup shredded coconut
½ cup chopped walnuts
1 to 2 tablespoons milk
2 cups sifted powdered sugar

In saucepan, melt ½ cup butter and 1 square unsweetened chocolate. Blend in sugar, egg, 1 teaspoon vanilla extract, graham cracker crumbs, coconut and walnuts. Mix well and press into ungreased 9x13-inch pan. Refrigerate. Mix together ¼ cup butter, milk, powdered sugar and remaining 1 teaspoon vanilla extract and spread over crumb mixture. Chill. Melt remaining unsweetened chocolate and remaining 1 teaspoon butter together. Spread evenly over chilled filling. Chill again. Cut into tiny squares before completely firm. Makes 4 to 5 dozen cookies.

Chocolate Clusters

1 (6-ounce) package semisweet chocolate bits
3 tablespoons light corn syrup
1 tablespoon water
1 cup grated coconut
½ cup chopped candied cherries

Melt together in top of double boiler chocolate bits, corn syrup and water. Add coconut and candied cherries. Drop by half teaspoonfuls onto aluminum foil and chill until firm. Makes 3 dozen.

Daffy Taffy

2 cups sugar
⅔ cup light corn syrup
⅓ cup water

2 tablespoons margarine
Flavoring (see list below)
Food coloring

Combine sugar, corn syrup, water and margarine in large saucepan. Bring to a boil over medium heat, stirring constantly, until sugar is dissolved. Continue to boil until mixture reaches firm-ball stage (242° to 248° on a candy thermometer). Remove from heat. Stir in desired flavorings and colorings. If making more than 1 flavor or color, divide mixture among 2 or 3 greased bowls before flavoring and coloring. Let taffy mixture stand until cool enough to handle. Pull taffy with well greased hands until it is light and no longer shiny. Stretch into a rope or coil about ½ inch in diameter; cut into ¾-inch pieces with scissors. Individually wrap candies in wax paper if desired. Store in airtight container. Makes 4 dozen pieces.

FLAVORING OPTIONS:

1½ teaspoons vanilla or fruit flavored extract
¼ teaspoon peppermint oil or fruit flavored oil

What is your favorite candy?

Name _____ Age _____

Finger Paint

½ cup cornstarch
3 tablespoons sugar
½ teaspoon salt
2 cups cold water
Food coloring

In a medium-size saucepan, mix all ingredients together. Cook over low heat 10 to 15 minutes, stirring with a wooden spoon, until mixture is smooth and thick. Remove from heat; cool. Divide mixture into small containers based on how many colors you want to use. Add a few drops food coloring to each container; stir. Continue adding food coloring 1 drop at a time and stirring well before deciding if you want to add more. Cover tightly to store.

Pioneer Strawberry Leather

This is a heritage recipe from our country's pioneers and is also a great way to use overripe fruit.

3 cups fresh strawberries
1 tablespoon lemon juice
1 tablespoon light corn syrup

Purée strawberries in a blender until smooth. Measure 2 cups purée (save any leftover for another use) and stir in lemon juice and corn syrup. Line a 15x10x1-inch jelly-roll pan with heavy plastic wrap and tape at corners. Spread strawberry mixture onto plastic, leaving 1-inch margins on all sides. Dry in a dehydrator or low oven (150°) 7 to 8 hours or until surface is dry and no longer sticky. Remove leather while still warm and tightly roll up from the narrow end. Cut into 5 (2-inch) logs and wrap securely with plastic. This is also terrific made with peaches, apples, bananas, apricots or a combination of fruits.

Fifteen Minute Mint Party Candy

6 red and green candy canes
1 (20-ounce) package white almond bark

Put unwrapped candy canes in a zip-close bag and crush with a hammer. Put 3 to 4 pieces of almond bark in a microwave-safe glass bowl and microwave until soft enough to stir (about 3 minutes; watch carefully). Stir some of the crushed candy canes into the melted bark. Spread mixture thinly over wax paper-lined cookie sheet and place in freezer 5 to 10 minutes. When firm, break candy into serving-size pieces as desired. Repeat until the right amount of candy for your occasion has been made.

Note: For other holidays, such as St. Patrick's Day, add a hint of green food coloring or green sprinkles to the melted bark along with the candy canes.

Gumdrops

2 tablespoon unflavored gelatin
½ cup cold water
2 cups sugar plus additional for rolling
¾ cup boiling water
Flavorings as desired
Food coloring

Soften gelatin in cold water. Combine 2 cups sugar and boiling water. Boil 5 minutes; add gelatin. Stir until dissolved. Boil slowly 15 minutes. Divide into 3 portions; flavor each portion and tint with desired food coloring. Pour into shallow pans which have been dipped in cold water. Let stand overnight. Turn out and cut in squares. Roll in sugar. Refrigerate until ready to eat.

Lollipops

2 cups sugar
⅔ cup light corn syrup
½ cup water
Flavorings (see list below)

Food coloring
Ribbons, lollipop sticks, or ice cream
 sticks
Small candies, optional

Using a wooden spoon, stir first 3 ingredients in saucepan over low heat until sugar is dissolved. Increase heat to high. Bring to boil, without stirring, and cook 15 to 20 minutes to hard-crack stage (300° to 310° on a candy thermometer). Remove from heat. Blend in desired flavoring and food coloring. Using your imagination, slowly pour different shapes onto a foil-lined baking sheet. Using back of spoon (careful, mixture is still very hot) immediately press ribbons or lollipop sticks into each shape. Decorate with small candies. Cool at room temperature.

FLAVOR OPTIONS:

1½ teaspoons peppermint extract
2 teaspoons lemon extract
½ teaspoon almond extract
¼ teaspoon oil of cinnamon
1 teaspoon vanilla extract

Stepping Stone

½ cup salt
½ cup flour
¼ cup water

Combine all ingredients. Knead until a stiff dough forms. Flatten to a round shape. Make an impression or draw a design. Bake at 200° for 3 hours. This is great for making hand- and/or footprints of your children. Make 1 every summer to see how the children have grown.

Cobblestones

3 (6-ounce) packages semisweet chocolate bits
2 cups miniature marshmallows
1 cup coarsely chopped walnuts

Line an 8-inch-square pan with foil. Melt chocolate bits in top of double boiler over hot water. Stir until smooth and add marshmallows and walnuts. Spread in prepared pan. Let stand until firm. Cut into squares. Makes 1⅔ pounds.

What is your favorite past time?

_____

Name_____

Age _____

What is your favorite cartoon?

Name

Age

Butterscotch-Oatmeal Cookies

1½ cups flour
1 teaspoon salt
¾ teaspoon baking soda
1 teaspoon cinnamon
1 cup sugar
¾ cup butter, softened
2 eggs
⅓ cup milk
1½ cups rolled oats
1 (6-ounce) package butterscotch bits
1 cup raisins
½ cup chopped walnuts

Sift together and set aside flour, salt, baking soda and cinnamon. Combine in bowl and beat until creamy sugar, butter and eggs. Gradually add flour mixture to creamed mixture alternately with milk. Stir in rolled oats, butterscotch bits, raisins and walnuts. Drop by tablespoonfuls onto greased cookie sheets. Bake at 350° for 12 to 14 minutes. Makes 5 dozen cookies.

Chocolate Chip Cookies

½ cup granulated sugar

½ cup packed brown sugar

¾ cup margarine or butter, softened

1 egg

1½ cups all-purpose flour

½ teaspoon baking soda

½ teaspoon salt

½ cup coarsely chopped nuts, optional

1 (6-ounce) package semisweet chocolate chips

Heat oven to 375°. Mix both sugars, margarine and egg in a large bowl with a wooden spoon. Stir in flour, baking soda and salt (dough will be stiff). Stir in nuts and chocolate chips. Drop by rounded tablespoonfuls onto an ungreased cookie sheet. Bake until light brown, 10 to 12 minutes. Let cookies cool slightly, and then remove from cookie sheet with a spatula. Makes about 24 cookies.

What is your favorite bedtime Story?

_____

Name_____

Age _____

Who reads it to you?

_____

Nitey-Nite Cookies

2 egg whites
⅔ cup sugar
1 cup chopped nuts
1 cup chocolate chips

Preheat oven to 350°. Beat egg whites until stiff, adding sugar gradually. Stir in nuts and chocolate chips. Drop by teaspoon on foil-lined cookie sheets. Put in oven and turn it off. Do not open until morning! Makes 4 dozen.

Name_____

Age _____

What is your favorite animal at the zoo?

Zebra Stripe Cookies

3 cups all-purpose flour
1 cup granulated sugar
¾ cup powdered sugar
1 teaspoon vanilla
1¼ cups butter, softened
¼ teaspoon salt
1 egg
¼ cup cocoa

Mix flour, sugars, vanilla, butter, salt and egg to form a dough. Divide dough in half. Mix cocoa into 1 half. Pat or roll each half into a 9-inch square. Cut each square into 3 (3-inch) strips. Cut strips crosswise in half. Place 1 brown strip onto plastic wrap. Top with 1 white strip; press firmly. Top with remaining strips, alternating colors and pressing firmly to form a bar. Wrap in plastic wrap and chill for 1 to 2 hours. Heat oven to 375°. Cut bar crosswise into about 18 (¼-inch) slices; cut each slice crosswise in half. Place on ungreased cookie sheet. Bake until edges begin to brown, 8 to 10 minutes. Makes 36 cookies.

What is your favorite time of year?

☐ Spring   ☐ Summer

☐ Fall   ☐ Winter

Lollipop Cookies

1 box rainbow chip cake mix
¾ cup water
2 eggs
20 to 24 wooden sticks with rounded ends
1 (16-ounce) tub creamy frosting

Heat oven to 375°. Beat cake mix, water and eggs in large bowl 30 seconds on low speed. Beat on high speed 2 minutes. Drop dough by rounded tablespoons 3 inches apart onto ungreased cookie sheet. Insert wooden sticks 1½ inches into edge of dough. Bake 8 to 11 minutes or until puffed and almost no indentation remains when touched. Cool 1 minute. Remove from cookie sheet and cool. Frost and decorate as desired. Makes 20 to 24 cookies.

Cake Mix Cookies

1 box yellow cake mix
2 eggs
1 stick margarine, melted
½ cup chocolate chips, chopped nuts and/or candy, optional
Powdered sugar

Mix dry cake mix with eggs and margarine. Add chips and/or nuts and candy of your choice, if desired. Drop by spoonfuls on cookie sheet and bake 10 minutes at 350°. Do not overcook. Sift powdered sugar over cookies.

Variation: Use flavored cake mix; lemon and strawberry are particularly good.

What is your favorite Bible Story?

_____

Name_____ Age_____

Best Brownies

1 cup butter
½ cup cocoa
2 cups all-purpose flour
2 cups sugar

4 eggs
4 teaspoons vanilla
1 cup chopped nuts, optional
Frosting, optional

Grease and flour a 9x13-inch baking pan. Melt butter in microwave and put into mixing bowl. Add cocoa and mix together until smooth. Add flour and sugar. Beat together and add eggs, vanilla and nuts. Mix until combined. Do not over stir. Batter will not be runny like a cake mix. Scrape into prepared pan and spread it out with a rubber spatula. Bake 20 to 25 minutes at 350° or until done. Frost brownies while still warm.

Do you know the stories of these people in the Bible?

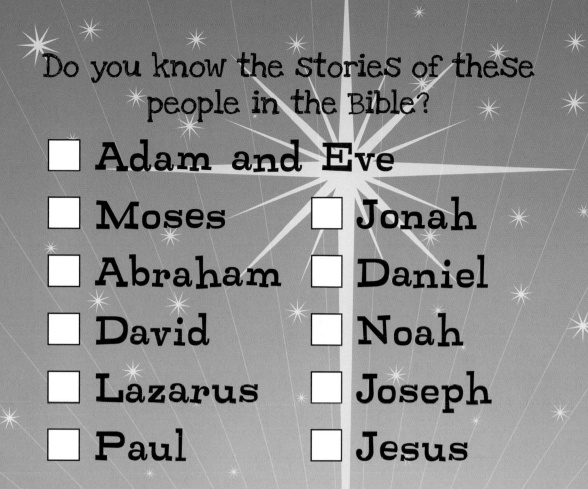

- [ ] Adam and Eve
- [ ] Moses
- [ ] Jonah
- [ ] Abraham
- [ ] Daniel
- [ ] David
- [ ] Noah
- [ ] Lazarus
- [ ] Joseph
- [ ] Paul
- [ ] Jesus

What color is your favorite pair of shoes?

_____

Name_____ Age_____

Banana Split Pie

1 (3-ounce) package cream cheese, softened
2 cups powdered sugar
1 graham cracker pie crust
1 (8-ounce) can crushed pineapple
2 medium bananas
1 (6-ounce) box instant white chocolate pudding and pie filling mix
1½ cups cold milk
1 (8-ounce) container Cool Whip
10 strawberries

Beat cream cheese and powdered sugar together until fluffy. Spread evenly over bottom of crust. Drain pineapple well and spread evenly over cream cheese. Slice bananas and cover pineapple with slices. Combine pudding and milk and beat about 2 minutes until thick. Pour over fruit. Top with whipped topping, covering entire pie, and garnish with strawberries or other fresh fruit.

Butter Chess Pie

2 cups sugar
2 tablespoons all-purpose flour
5 large eggs, lightly beaten
⅔ cup buttermilk
½ cup butter or margarine, melted
1 teaspoon vanilla
1 (9-inch) pastry shell, unbaked

Heat oven to 350°. In large bowl, combine sugar and flour; stir in eggs and buttermilk until blended. Add butter and vanilla. Pour filling into pastry shell and bake 45 minutes or until set. Check for doneness after the minimum baking time by gently shaking the pie. The center should be set with a slight jiggle. Cool on wire rack.

Which team do you like to cheer for?

_____

Which sport they play?

_____

Name _____

Age _____

Lemonade Pie

This is an easy recipe yet makes a deliciously creamy pie and it is just as good made with limeade.

1 (6-ounce) can frozen lemonade

1 (14-ounce) can sweetened condensed milk

1 (8-ounce) container Cool Whip or whipped cream, plus more
   for serving

1 graham cracker crust, homemade or store bought

Use mixer and mix all ingredients except crust until fluffy. Pour into pie crust. Refrigerate several hours or overnight until firm. Top with additional whipped topping and garnish with lemon slices.

Butterfinger Pie

6 (2.125-ounce) Butterfinger candy bars, crushed

1 (8-ounce) package cream cheese, softened

1 (12-ounce) carton Cool Whip

1 graham cracker pie crust

Mix first 3 ingredients together and pour into pie crust. Chill before serving.

List some things you like to do.

_____

Name_____

Age_____

Chocolate Cobbler

COBBLER:

¾ cup sugar

1 cup self-rising flour

2 tablespoons cocoa

½ cup milk

3 tablespoons melted butter

1 teaspoon vanilla

TOPPING:

½ cup sugar

½ cup brown sugar

¼ cup cocoa

Mix Cobbler ingredients together and spread in a greased 11x7-inch or 9x13-inch glass baking dish. Mix Topping ingredients together and sprinkle evenly over Cobbler mixture. Pour 1½ cups hot water gently over all. Do not mix; just gently pour over all. Bake at 350° for 40 minutes. Serve hot or cold.

Baker's Clay Ornaments

⅓ cup water
½ cup salt
1 cup flour
Foil
Sharpened pencil
Poster paint
Brushes
Shellac or varnish
Yarn

Mix water, salt and flour in a bowl with your hands to form clay. Take bits of the clay and make different shapes. Place on a baking sheet covered with foil. Make a hole in the top of each shape with the point of a pencil. Bake at 275° for 1 hour, until brown. Let shapes cool and then paint them. When paint is dry, coat with shellac or varnish. String with yarn and hang on your tree.

Chocolate Pizza

1 (12-ounce) package semisweet chocolate chips
16 ounces white almond bark, divided
2 cups miniature marshmallows
1 cup crisp rice cereal
1 cup salted roasted peanuts
1 (6-ounce) jar red maraschino cherries, drained and halved
2 tablespoons green maraschino cherries, drained and quartered
⅓ cup flaked coconut
1 teaspoon oil, optional

Microwave chocolate chips and 14 ounces of almond bark at medium until smooth. Stir in marshmallows, cereal and peanuts. Pour onto lightly greased 12-inch pizza pan. Top with cherries and sprinkle with coconut. Microwave remaining almond bark and oil at medium until smooth. Drizzle over pizza. Refrigerate until firm. Store at room temperature. Chips and almond bark may be melted on stovetop over low heat if desired.

Variations: Substitute red and green M&M's for the cherries, walnuts or pecans for the peanuts, and Chinese noodles for the coconut. You can also make 2 or 3 smaller pizzas or shape foil into a heart, tree, shamrock, etc., for different occasions.

Chocolate Peanut Butter Crescents

CRESCENTS:
¼ cup peanut butter chips
¼ cup milk chocolate chips
¼ cups finely chopped nuts
1 (8-ounce) can refrigerated quick crescent dinner rolls
Powdered sugar or Peanut Butter Chocolate Drizzle

Heat oven to 375°. Stir together chips and nuts in small bowl. Unroll dough to form 8 triangles. Lightly sprinkle 1 heaping tablespoon chip mixture over each triangle; gently press into dough. Starting at widest end of triangle, roll dough to point. Place rolls, point side down, on ungreased cookie sheet; curve into crescent shape. Bake 10 to 12 minutes or until golden brown. Sift powdered sugar over the top or drizzle with Peanut Butter Chocolate Drizzle.

PEANUT BUTTER CHOCOLATE DRIZZLE:
¼ cup peanut butter chips
¼ cup milk chocolate chips
1 teaspoon shortening (do not substitute)

Place chips and shortening in small microwave-safe bowl. Microwave on high (100% power) 30 seconds; stir. If necessary, microwave an additional 15 seconds at a time, stirring after each heating, just until chips are melted when stirred.

Edible Aquarium

1 (3-ounce) package
Jell-O Berry Blue
Gelatin Dessert
¾ cup boiling water

½ cup cold water
Ice cubes
Gummy fish

Dissolve gelatin completely in boiling water. Combine cold water and ice cubes to make 1¼ cups. Add to gelatin, stirring until slightly thickened. Remove any unmelted ice cubes. If mixture is still thin, refrigerate until slightly thickened. Pour thickened gelatin into 4 dessert dishes. Suspend gummy fish in gelatin. Refrigerate until set, about 1 hour.

What do you like to do at the beach?

_____

Have you ever seen a jellyfish?

☐ **Yes**   ☐ **No**

Have you built a sand castle?

☐ **Yes**   ☐ **No**

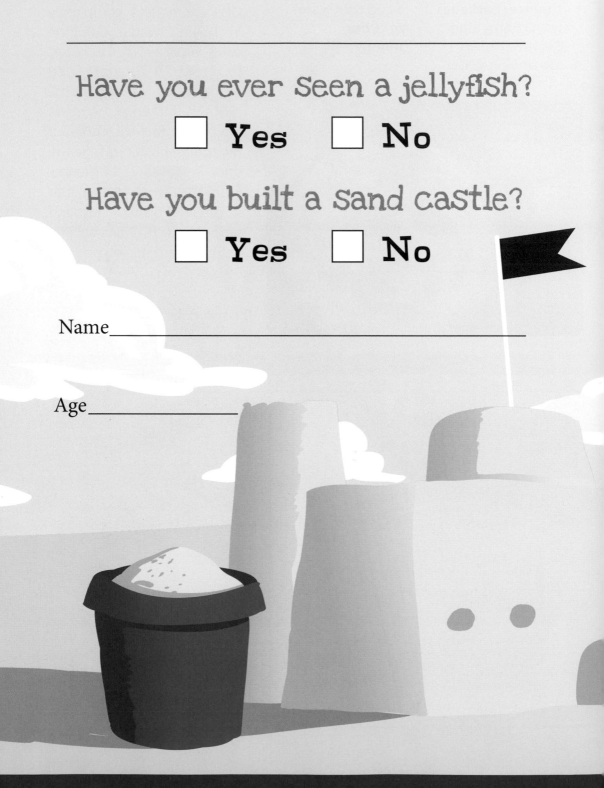

Name_____

Age_____

Flapjack Party Stack

1 box yellow cake mix, plus ingredients to prepare
1 (16-ounce) container vanilla frosting
1 quart fresh strawberries, washed, hulled and sliced
1 cup caramel or butterscotch ice cream topping

Preheat oven to 350°. Grease bottoms and sides of 4 (9-inch) round cake pans; line bottoms with wax paper. Prepare and bake cake mix according to package directions. Let cakes cool in pans on wire racks 15 minutes. Remove from pans; cool completely. Reserve ¼ cup frosting. Place 1 cake layer on serving plate; spread or pipe one third of remaining frosting in swirls on cake to resemble whipped butter. Top with one quarter of sliced strawberries. Repeat with next 2 cake layers, frosting and strawberries. Top stack with remaining cake layer. Warm caramel topping in microwave just until pourable. Drizzle over cake. Spread or pipe reserved frosting in center; garnish with remaining strawberries. Makes 12 servings.

Homemade Wrapping Paper

Cookie cutters or foam shapes
Paint
Tissue paper

Dip bottoms of cookie cutters or foam shapes into paint and gently stamp onto tissue paper. Let dry.

What is your favorite TV show?

_____

Name_____

Age_____

Pail of Dirt

14 Oreo cookies
2 cups cold milk
Children's sand pail and shovel
1 (3.9-ounce) package chocolate instant pudding
Wire whisk
1½ cups Cool Whip
Gummy worms and gummy frogs for decorations

Crush cookies in plastic bag with rolling pin. Pour milk into pail. Add pudding mix. Beat with wire whisk until well blended, 1 to 2 minutes. Let stand 5 minutes or until thickened.

Stir in whipped topping. Gradually stir in 1 cup crushed cookies. Top with remaining crushed cookies. Refrigerate until ready to serve. Decorate with gummy worms and gummy frogs just before serving with shovel.

Simple Farmhouse Rice Pudding

2 cups cooked rice
½ cups sugar
2 eggs, slightly beaten
2 cups milk
½ teaspoon vanilla
½ teaspoon cinnamon,
  optional

Place rice in bowl. Add remaining ingredients, except cinnamon, and stir to mix. Pour into greased 2-quart baking dish. Sprinkle with cinnamon if desired. Bake about 25 minutes at 350° until set.

Peanut Butter Pudding

This is a high-protein, low-sugar dessert.

1 banana, cut into chunks
½ cup plain yogurt
½ cup peanut butter

Combine all ingredients in blender container. Blend until smooth. Pour into serving dishes and refrigerate an hour, or longer, before serving. Makes 2 servings.

Ice Cream Sandwiches

½ cup granulated sugar

½ cup packed brown sugar

½ cup peanut butter

¼ cup shortening, softened, plus 2 tablespoons, divided

¼ cup margarine or butter, softened

1 egg

1¼ cups all-purpose flour

¾ teaspoon baking soda

½ teaspoon baking powder

¼ teaspoon salt

1 pint ice cream (any flavor), slightly softened

1 (6-ounce) package semisweet chocolate chips

Heat oven to 375°. Beat both sugars, peanut butter, ¼ cup shortening and margarine until combined. Beat in egg. Mix flour, baking soda, baking powder and salt together and blend into sugar mixture. Shape into 1¼-inch balls. Place 3 inches apart on cookie sheet. Bake until brown, 9 to 11 minutes. Cool.

For each ice cream sandwich, press 1 slightly rounded tablespoon of ice cream between 2 cookies; Place in jelly-roll pan. Freeze until firm. Melt chips and 2 tablespoons shortening, stirring occasionally. Let stand 2 minutes. Dip half of each sandwich into chocolate. Place back in pan; freeze until firm. Store wrapped in plastic wrap. Makes 15.

Cookie Sundae Cups

1 (18-ounce) package refrigerated chocolate chip cookie
  dough
6 cups ice cream, any flavor
1¼ cups ice cream topping, any flavor
Whipped cream
Colored sprinkles

Preheat oven to 350°. Lightly grease 18 (2½-inch) muffin pan cups. Remove dough from wrapper. Shape dough into 18 balls; press onto bottoms and up sides of prepared muffin cups. Bake 14 to 18 minutes or until golden brown. Cool in pan 10 minutes. Remove cups from pan and cool completely on wire rack. Divide ice cream between cookie cups (about ⅓ cup each). Drizzle with ice cream topping. Top with whipped cream and colored sprinkles.

All-American Sundae

1 large scoop raspberry
  sherbet
1 large scoop vanilla ice
  cream
½ cup blueberries
2 tablespoons whipped
  cream
1 maraschino cherry

Place sherbet in tall glass or sundae dish. Add vanilla ice cream. Top with blueberries and whipped cream. Place cherry on top.

Single-Serving Ice Cream in a Bag

This recipe has been around a long time; I remember doing this back in school when I was little. When I make it with my kids, they are amazed at how fast it is.

2 tablespoons sugar
1 cup half-and-half or light cream
½ teaspoon vanilla extract
1 pint-size zip-close plastic bag
Ice cubes
½ cup coarse salt or table salt
1 gallon-size zip-close plastic bag

Combine sugar, half-and-half and vanilla extract in a 2- to 4-cup measuring cup. Pour into a pint-size plastic bag and seal. (Make sure it seals tightly.) Fill a gallon-size bag halfway with ice cubes; pour salt over ice. Place cream-filled bag into ice-filled bag and seal tightly. Shake 5 to 8 minutes. Open gallon-size bag and check to see if ice cream is hard. If not, reseal and shake a little longer. Once ice cream is hard, quickly run closed pint-size bag under cold water to clean salt off. Open the bag and pop in a spoon. It is so much fun for each child to make (and eat!) their own ice cream.

Happy Ice Cream Mice

2 cups vanilla ice cream

1 (4-ounce) package single-serving graham cracker crusts

6 chocolate sandwich cookies, separated and cream filling removed

12 black jelly beans

6 red jelly beans

36 chocolate sprinkles (approximately ¼ teaspoon)

Place 1 rounded scoop (about ⅓ cup) ice cream into each crust. Freeze 10 minutes. Press 1 cookie half into each side of ice cream scoops for ears. Decorate with black jelly beans for eyes, red jelly beans for noses and chocolate sprinkles for whiskers. Freeze 10 minutes before serving. Makes 6 servings.

Fudgesicles

1 cup sugar

1 (3.4-ounce) package chocolate fudge pudding mix (cook and serve; not instant)

3 cups cold milk

1 (8-ounce) carton Cool Whip

Popsicle sticks

Mix sugar, pudding mix and milk in saucepan. Cook as directed for making pudding. Cool. Blend in whipped topping. Put mixture in any size paper cups you desire. Place in freezer. When partially frozen, insert a Popsicle stick into middle of each cup. Freeze until firm. Refreshing and easy.

Almond Fudge Pops

1 (1.3-ounce) envelope Dream Whip

½ cup cold milk

½ teaspoon vanilla extract

¾ cup hot fudge ice cream topping

2 tablespoons water

1 cup toasted, finely chopped almonds, divided

6 (3-ounce) disposable plastic cups

6 popsicle sticks

In a bowl, beat topping mix, milk and vanilla extract on low speed until blended. Beat on high until soft peaks form, about 4 minutes. In a large bowl, combine fudge topping and water. Add to Dream Whip mixture with ½ cup almonds. Pour into plastic cups. Cover with heavy-duty foil; insert sticks through foil. Place in a 9-inch square pan. Freeze until firm. Remove foil and cups. Roll frozen pops in remaining almonds.

Who is your best friend?

_____

What do you do together?

_____

Name_____ Age_____

Cherry-Lemonade Pops

1 (10-ounce) jar maraschino cherries
8 (3-ounce) paper cups
1 (12-ounce) can frozen pink lemonade
  concentrate, partially thawed
¼ cup water
8 Popsicle sticks

Drain cherries, reserving juice. Place 1 whole cherry in each paper cup. Coarsely chop remaining cherries. Add chopped cherries, lemonade concentrate, water and reserved juice to blender or food processor; blend until smooth. Fill paper cups with equal amounts of cherry mixture. Freeze several hours or until very slushy. Place Popsicle sticks into center of each cup. Freeze 1 hour longer or until firm. To serve, peel off paper cups.

Note: Serve immediately after peeling off the paper cups; these pops melt very quickly.

Banana Sicles

Fun for the kids to monkey around making.

Banana
Orange juice
Chopped nuts

Peel banana; pierce lengthwise with a Popsicle stick. Dip banana in orange juice. Roll in chopped nuts. Freeze.

Fruit Popsicles

¼ to ½ watermelon, cut in chunks and seeded ½ cup fresh blueberries
½ cup chopped fresh strawberries
1 kiwi fruit, peeled and chopped
1 peach or nectarine, diced small
Handful fresh cherries, pitted and chopped
Popsicle molds

Purée seeded watermelon in blender until smooth to make 3 cups puree. Set aside. Mix fruits together. Set out about 1 dozen Popsicle molds. Fill each mold with the mixed fresh fruit. Pour watermelon purée into each mold until full to the top. Place a Popsicle stick into each mold. Freeze 6 to 8 hours. When ready to serve, run molds under warm water a few seconds and remove Popsicles.

Creamy Strawberry-Orange Pops

1 (8-ounce) container strawberry-flavored yogurt
¾ cup orange juice
2 teaspoons vanilla
2 cups frozen whole strawberries
2 teaspoons sugar
6 (7-ounce) paper cups
6 wooden sticks

Combine yogurt, orange juice and vanilla in food processor or blender; process until smooth. Add frozen strawberries and sugar substitute; process until smooth. Pour into paper cups, filling each about three-quarters full. Place in freezer 1 hour. Insert wooden stick into center of each cup. Freeze completely. Peel cup off each pop before serving.

what is your favorite lip-gloss flavor?

Name_____

Age _____

Activities

Can you find this picture somewhere in the book?

Page _____

Memories

Can you find this picture somewhere in the book?

Page _____

Index of Recipes

Can you find this picture somewhere in the book?

Page _____

Can you find this picture
somewhere in the book?

Page _____

Can you find this picture
somewhere in the book?

Page _____

Can you find this picture somewhere in the book?

Page _____

Can you find these pictures somewhere in the book?

Page _____

Page _____

Page _____

Page _____

Page _____

Page _____

Can you find these pictures somewhere in the book?

Page _____

Page _____

Page _____

Page _____

Page _____

Page _____

Image Credits

Images ©James Stefuik: **p9**: Ocean in a Bottle • **p25**: Egg Sailboats • **p60**: Flubber • **p108**: Balloon Creations • **p121**: Monster Mouths • **p127**: Trivets • **p142**: Hand Print • **p158**: Popcorn Cake • **p168**: Magic Balloon Treats • **p170**: Dirt Cake • **p178**: Oreo Brownie Cupcakes • **p181**: Frog Cupcakes • **p198**: Finger Paint • **p202**: Stepping Stone • **p220**: Baker's Clay Ornaments • **p223**: Edible Aquarium • **p226**: Homemade Wrapping Paper • **p228**: Pail of Dirt • **p233**: Happy Ice Cream Mice

Images © istock.com by the creator noted unless otherwise noted.

FRONT: p1: mixing bowls, billnoll • **p2**: girl chef, Dejan Ristovski • **p3**: marble specks, lucato; index card, paladaxar; measuring spoons, gardendata • **p4-5**: gray marble, lucato • **p6**: smiling spoon, artlensfoto • **p7**: gold laminate countertop, Roel Smart

BEVERAGES & SNACKS: p8: flame, muzzza; cider sign, EdwardSamuelCornwall; Apple Worm, ChinHooi • **p9**: ocean waves, IkonStudio; pirate ship, PinkPueblo • **p10**: lemonade stand, JimVallee; wood table, kwasny221; lemon faces, serazetdinov • **p11**: orange, anna1311; orange splatter, lianella; peppermint stick, polesnoy • **p12**: snowflakes, Padrinan; Purple cowgirl, clipartdotcom • **p13**: santa letter, frankiefotografie; swirl candy, yganko; pinefir tree, RonyZmiri; paper ornament, vesmil • **p14**: principal, nito100 • **p15**: chalkboard misbehave, klikk; blank notebook, wildpixel • **p16-17**: patriotic background, CobaltMoon; states, CobaltMoon; Texas badge, Stocki2000; boy guitar, lovleah; garbage, Moriz89 • **p18-19**: tortilla wrap, ffolas; tortilla chips, mayakova; chili peppers, maxicam • **p20**: dog food, marekuliasz; cat, pwollinga; tortoise, Nneirda; grass turf, cherezoff; corn dogs, Torsakarin • **p21**: dog blanket, igorr1 • **p22**: heart pizza, zitramon; chopping board, andylid • **p23**: checked swatch, petekarici; white napkin, didecs; pizza faces, bernashafo • **p24**: occupations, Rawpixel Ltd • **p25**: sail boat, WSS • **p26**: log, owattaphotos; grunge green, Nik_Merkulov; red ant, Suljo • **p27**: crystal mountains, katyau; butterfly, clairevis; daisies, sekerlili • **p28**: cloud raindrops, ClaudioVentrella • **p29**: handyman boy, inarik • **p30**: inflatable rings, yelet; boy underwater, shalamov; sun balloon, yurakr • **p31**: vacation car, Alias-Ching; vacation kids, SerrNovik; • **p32**: teddy bear heart, wahahaz • **p33**: chattering teeth, WestLight; brontosaurus, yayayoyo; Mud, topshotUK • **p34**: brown paper, robynmac; movie background, Yuriy Tsirkunov; television, scanrail; movie theater, agencyby; DVDs, kiev4 • **p35**: popcorn scatter, tanjichica7; popcorn bag, Lisovskaya; salt shake, robynmac; butter sliced, SvetlanaK

BREAD & BREAKFAST: p36-37: bananas, Naddiya; monkey selfie, hayaship; coconut monkey, AVNphotolab • **p38**: teddy bear, daniel_wiedemann • **p39**: dancing beans, Creative_Outlet; pig, kim_zhai; bean toast, robynmac • **p40-41**: Scrabble letters, Rena-Marie; board game, colematt • **p42**: ice cream cones, perkmeup; ice cream sprinkles, funkybg • **p43**: blueberry face, Elenathewise; strawberry background, zaporozsky • **p44**: ballerina room, KhongkitWiriyachan • **p45**: baby room, barsik • **p46**: happy toast, victoria_cartwright • **p47**: raised hands, Rawpixel Ltd • **p48**: French toast sticks, bhofack2 • **p49**: honey bear, dawnamoore; honeycomb background, tashechka • **p50**: pancakes, Marie Fields • **p51**: rabbit cooking pancake, Alexeyzet; strawberry cartoon, hanaschwarz • **p52**: friends running, monkeybusinessimages • **p53**: wafer background, ZlatkoGuzmic; heart waffles, nvelichko; chocolate chips, nata_vkusidey • **p54**: roasting marshmallows, Luke Miller • **p55**: blue sky, Anon_Pichit; smiling sun, Nasared; breakfast burrito, Bob Randall • **p56**: egg faces, lucato • **p57**: spring bulbs, natianis • **p58**: egg in hole, Yulia_Davidovich • **p59**: putting green, bennyb; hole in one trophy, Lisalson

SOUPS, SALADS & SANDWICHES: p60: green wave, cundra • **p61**: mixed vegetables, Danicek; electric cooker, design56 • **p62**: rainbow dots, MariaTkach • **p63**: girl in closet, Maya23K • **p64-65**: Ferris wheel, Jui-Chi Chan • **p66**: apple rings, hydrangea100; red ribbon, fotohunter • **p67**: flower vegetables, Cristian Gabrie Kerekes • **p68-69**: kite, perrineweets; rainbow, zirui01; crayons, empire331 • **p70**: polar bear, Lanaufoto; frozen grapes, JulNichols • **p71**: puppy bunny ears, Fly_dragonfly • **p72**: superhero, rudall30; super pow, wissanu99 • **p73**: child superhero, Tomwang112 • **p74**: bun, TimArbaev; sports ball, wildpixel • **p75**: sports icons, tarras79 • **p76-77**: white bread, donatas1205; cheese slice, sparkia • **p78**: smiley balloon, st-design • **p79**: boy heart, Nadezhda1906

VEGETABLES & SIDE DISHES: p80: plasticine, AlexStar; plasticine monkey, imetlion; alphabet, Ajevs • **p81**: potato head, IvonneW; baking potato, ottoshtekker • **p82**: Foil, OSVALDRU; foil potatoes, LeeAnnWhite • **p83**: potato chips, Nik_Merkulov • **p84-85**: girl reading, mg7 • **p86**: hair scissors, pakornkrit • **p87**: mohawk hairstyle, ineb1599 • **p88**: zucchini cartoon, yayayoyo • **p89**: sweet potatoes, marrakeshh • **p90-91**: swiss cheese, shutswis; orange face, akiwi; sauerkraut, marekuliasz; broccoli, Dizzy; yuck! vegetables, inspireme; like and unlike symbols, digitalgenetics • **p92-93**: playing video games, diego_cervo; pixel pals, chuntise • **p94**: cabbage, morningarage; ceramic bunny, Tuned_In • **p95**: rabbits maze game, ksenya_savva • **p96**: buttered corn, MargoeEdwards • **p97**: cauliflower brain, akinshin; head silhouette, frikota • **p98-99**: praying hands, ChristinLola • **p100-101**: skateboarding, lzf; girls dance pose, mandygodbehear • **p102**: macaroni, mstroz; macaroni cheese cartoon, aoshlick • **p103**: tortilla stack, ericb007 • **p104**: businessman, AntonioGuillem • **p105**: blue collar worker, milla1974 • **p106**: peas, pxel66; vegetable face, KatarzynaBialasiewicz • **p107**: asparagus crown, valbar

BEEF & PORK: p109: balloon animals, SteveCollender; orange balloon, klikk • **p110-111**: castle silhouette, Tribalium; silhouette princess, yelet • **p112-113**: Hamburger fries, WestLight • **p114-115**: plaques, ayzek; student trophy, michaeljung • **p116**: hedgehog, luamduan • **p117**: green slime, solarseven; spider web, muuraa; green fly, pepeemilio; gummy worm, martaemg; mushy peas, lleerogers; kissing emoticons, yayayoyo; boy picking nose, naumoid • **p118-119**: girl cooking, AVolke • **p120-121**: Halloween silhouette, lianella • **p122-123**: Halloween pumpkins, IvanMikhaylov • **p124**: nurse, idrutu • **p125**: office worker, seiki14 • **p126**: sombrero and piñata, miflippo • **p127**: watercolor background, OttoKrause • **p128**: sprinkler, XiXinXing • **p129**: girl swinging, tepic • **p130**: empty plate, Nastco; vintage fork, Stepan_Bormotov; scalloped potatoes, Bronwyn8 • **p131**: boy with tablet, Zurijeta • **p132-133**: submarine, AnsyAgeeva • **p134-135**: barbecue on fire, toonerman

CHICKEN: p136-137: colorful background, hakkiarslan; bubble, snake3d; brown hen, alanholden; rotten egg, cthoman • **p138-139**: moving car, hxdyl; car keys, furtaev • **p140**: cardboard tv, ValeriKimbro • **p141**: block toy hen, Lalith_Herath • **p142-143**: color hand prints, portarefortuna • **p144-145**: kitchen sink, didecs; chicken tenders, aoshlick • **p146-147**: traveler girl, phaitoons • **p148-149**: bass drum, herreid • **p150-151**: teacher in classroom, AVAVA • **p152**: yellow suitcase, phaitoons • **p153**: senorita chicken, bobash • **p154-155**: hide-n-seek, sonyae

CAKES: p156: hummingbird, Kevin_LS • **p157**: hummingbird cake, Aiselin82 • **p158-159**: Sparklers, Evgeniya_m • **p160**: chocolate cake, plumchutney • **p161**: electric mixer, peredniankina • **p162-163**: singing cake, J-Dunbar; mp3 player, adisa; orange headphones, servickuz • **p164-165**: cola splash, Irochka_T; red can, Roman Samokhin; red paper cup, Coprid • **p166**: dear Santa, frankiefotografie; gingerbread cookies, MariuszBlach • **p167**: Christmas present, MariuszBlach • **p168-169**: balloons and confetti, YuriyS • **p170**: grass and soil, Okea • **p171**: bugs in bottle, mstay • **p172-173**: kids playing, Janista • **p174**: Ice cream cone cake, Yann Poirier • **p175**: white dress, SerrNovik • **p176-177**: party pets, adogslifephoto • **p178**: wood panel, Weedezign • **p179**: chocolate muffins, Chiociolla; spider webs, paprikaa • **p180-181**: water lilies, Marina_Morozova; frog, egal; clay frog, Bombaert; plasticine frog, imetlion; white cloud, phloxii; blue clay, Lesha

COOKIES & CANDIES: p182: breakfast cereal, Ericlefrancais • **p183**: cardboard box, ferlistockphoto • **p184**: starry sky, RossellaApostoli; Meteorite, AlexBannykh; asteroids, cthoman • **p185**: telescope silhouette, RossellaApostoli; child astronaut, McIninch; shooting star, ajt • **p186**: girl with binoculars, LydiaGoolia • **p187**: nest with eggs, SergeyChayko • **p188**: birds maze game, ratselmeister • **p189**: bird house, anankkml; chickadee, Ulga • **p190**: pecan turtles, Purestock • **p191**: old cabin in trees, DWalker44; pecans, Peter Zijlstra • **p192-193**: magician background, FreeTransform; child magician, TRITOOTH • **p194-195**: chocolate drips, macrovector • **p196**: taffy, rimglow • **p197**: holding candy, kirza • **p198-199**: finger painting, crosstudio • **p200**: gum drops, Somus • **p201**: turkey lollipops, aqabiz; lollipops, mayakova • **p202-203**: walking on stones, BrianAJackson • **p204**: boom explosion, Yakovliev; ninja kick, memoangeles; cartoon girl, caborial • **p205**: cookies and milk, Enjoylife2 • **p206**: girl reading, ozgurcoskun • **p207**: boy sleeping, BrianAJackson • **p208-209**: zoo animals, RossellaApostoli • **p210-211**: dandelion field, designnatures; four seasons, MartinaVaculikova • **p212-213**: star of Bethlehem, fogbird; Bible kids, PhotoEstelar

PIES & OTHER DESSERTS: p214: children's shoes, Garry518 • **p215**: baby shoes, egal • **p216-217**: foam finger, miflippo; stadium, Kalawin; dog cheerleader, WilleeCole • **p218-219**: riding bikes, SerrNovik • **p220**: star and bear ornaments, gimagphoto; clay hand, Alysta • **p221**: chocolate hands, Ella_ • **p222-223**: goldfish tank, mg7 • **p224-225**: sandcastle, DamonAce • **p226**: tissue paper background, czarny_bez • **p227**: kid watching tv, djedzura • **p228**: sand toys dirt, Egorius • **p229**: red barn, 4nadia • **p230-231**: bare feet, yaruta • **p232**: vanilla ice cream, egal • **p233**: happy mouse, vectorcartoons • **p234**: fudge popsicles, Lauri Patterson • **p235**: kids smartphone, nensuria • **p236**: yellow popsicle, Tuned_In • **p237**: homemade popsicles, MaximShebeko • **p238**: pink lipstick, tokhiti • **p239**: dress-up, AnnWorthy

Can you find this picture somewhere in the book?

Page _____

State Hometown Cookbook Series

A Hometown Taste of America, One State at a Time.

Each state's hometown charm is revealed through local recipes from real hometown cooks along with stories and photos that will take you back to your hometown . . . or take you on a journey to explore other hometowns across the country.

EACH: $18.95 • 240 to 272 pages • 8x9 • paperbound

Georgia	South Carolina	Texas
Louisiana	Tennessee	West Virginia
Mississippi		

Eat & Explore Cookbook Series

Discover community celebrations and unique destinations, as they share their favorite recipes.

Experience our United States like never before when you explore the distinct flavor of each state by savoring 250 favorite recipes from the state's best cooks. In addition, the state's favorite events and destinations are profiled throughout the book with fun stories and everything you need to know to plan your family's next road trip.

EACH: $18.95 • 240 to 272 pages • 7x9 • paperbound

Arkansas	Ohio	Virginia
Minnesota	Oklahoma	Washington
North Carolina		

State Back Road Restaurants Series

Every road leads to delicious food.

From two-lane highways and interstates, to dirt roads and quaint downtowns, every road leads to delicious food when traveling across our United States. The STATE BACK ROAD RESTAURANTS COOKBOOK SERIES serves up a well-researched and charming guide to each state's best back road restaurants. No time to travel? No problem. Each restaurant shares with you their favorite recipes—sometimes their signature dish, sometimes a family favorite, but always delicious.

EACH: $18.95 • 256 pages • 7x9 • paperbound • full-color

Alabama • Kentucky • Tennessee • Texas

www.GreatAmericanPublishers.com • www.facebook.com/GreatAmericanPublishers

It's So Easy...

Kitchen Memories Cookbook
Your Recipe for Family Fun in the Kitchen

This kids' cookbook and free-style memory book guarantees hours of fun and a lifetime of memories for your family.

It's a cookbook, a memory book, and an activity book—all in one! So grab a kid, head to the kitchen, and start making your own Kitchen Memories.

A cherished keepsake for your family.

Makes a great gift!

$18.95 • 256 pages • 7x10 • paperbound • full-color

Family Favorite Recipes

It's so easy to cook great food your family will love with 350 simply delicious recipes for easy-to-afford, easy-to-prepare dinners. From **Great Grandmother's Coconut Pie**, to **Granny's Vanilla Wafer Cake** to **Mama's Red Beans & Rice**, this outstanding cookbook is the result of decades of cooking and collecting recipes. It's so easy to encourage your family to eat more meals at home…to enjoy time spent in the kitchen… to save money making delicious affordable meals…to cook the foods your family loves without the fuss…with *Family Favorite Recipes*.

$18.95 • 248 pages • 7x10 • paperbound • full-color

Don't miss out on our upcoming titles—join our Cookbook Club and you'll be notified of each new edition.

www.GreatAmericanPublishers.com • toll-free 1-888-854-5954

ORDER FORM
Mail to: Great American Publishers • 171 Lone Pine Church Road • Lena, MS 39094
Or call us toll-free 1.888.854.5954 to order by check or credit card

❑ Check Enclosed
Charge to: ❑ Visa ❑ MC ❑ AmEx ❑ Disc

Card # _____

Exp Date Signature _____

Name _____

Address _____

City/State _____

Zip _____

Phone _____

Email _____

Qty.	Title	Total
	Subtotal	

Postage ($3.50 first book; $1.00 each additional;
Order 4 or more books, FREE SHIPPING) _____

Total _____